DESTIN TRAVEL GUIDE

Unveiling Emerald Coast Adventure, Beaches & Hidden Gem

Vera Shears

Copyright © Vera Shears 2024. All rights reserved

This work and its content are protected under international copyright laws. No part of this work may be reproduced, distributed, or transmitted in any form or by any means, including photocopying, recording, or other electronic or mechanical methods, without the prior written permission of the copyright holder, except in the case of brief quotations embodied in critical reviews and certain other noncommercial uses permitted by copyright law.

Disclaimer

The information provided in **Destin Guide 2024: Unveiling Emerald Coast Adventure, Beaches & Hidden Gem,** is for general informational purposes only. While every effort has been made to ensure the accuracy and completeness of the content, the author, publisher, and contributors assume no responsibility for errors, inaccuracies, omissions, or any outcomes related to the use of this information.

Travel conditions, business operations, and services mentioned in this book are subject to change. Readers are encouraged to verify any information, such as opening hours, availability of activities, and travel advisories, before making any travel plans or reservations. The inclusion of any venue, business, or service does not imply endorsement by the author or publisher.

Health and safety guidelines should be followed at all times. The author, publisher, and contributors are not liable for any loss, injury, or inconvenience sustained by anyone using this guide. Activities mentioned in this book, including but not limited to water sports, hiking, and dining experiences, carry inherent risks, and it is the responsibility of the reader to undertake appropriate precautions and make informed decisions.

This book is intended to enhance your travel experience and provide recommendations based on current knowledge and personal experiences. However, the dynamic nature of the travel industry means that some information may become outdated. The author and publisher encourage readers to conduct further research and exercise their best judgment when planning their travel itinerary.

By using this guide, you agree to hold harmless the author, publisher, and contributors from any claims, damages, or liabilities arising from your use of the information provided. Enjoy your journey responsibly and savor the wonders of Destin with the confidence that comes from being an informed traveler.

Safe trip and happy adventures!

TABLE OF CONTENTS

ABOUT THE BOOK 7

INTRODUCTION 9

    Overview of Destin 10

    How To Use This Guide 19

    Getting There 21

    When Should You Visit? 24

1. EPIC ADVENTURES 28

    1.1 Water Activities 28

    1.2 Land-based Thrills 39

2. MUST-SEE SIGHTS 44

    2.1 Beaches and Parks 44

    2.2 Historic and Cultural Sites 49

    2.3 Scenic Locations 56

3. HIDDEN GEMS 69

    3.1 Off the Beaten Path Beaches 69

    3.2 Unique Attractions 73

3.4 Best-Kept Secret Restaurants 87

4. RELAXATION & WELLNESS 95

    4.1 Spa and Wellness Centres 95

    4.2 Mindfulness Activities 106

5: FAMILY FUN 111

    5.1 Kids-Friendly Beaches in Destin 111

    5.2 Family attractions 116

    5.3 Educational Experiences 122

6: DINING AND NIGHTLIFE 128

    6.1 The Top Restaurants in Destin 128

    6.2 Must-Try Local Cuisine 135

    6.3 Destiny After Dark 141

7: SHOPPING 148

    7.1 Destin's Premier Shopping Districts 148

    7.2 Destin's Markets and Festivals 159

8: Practical Information 165

    8.1 Accommodations in Destin 165

    8.2 Getting Around Destin 171

ABOUT THE BOOK

Welcome to **Destin Travel Guide:** Unveiling Emerald Coast Adventure, Beaches & Hidden Gem

This book is your key to discovering one of Florida's most captivating coastal towns, a place where emerald waters meet sugar-white sands and every moment holds the promise of adventure and relaxation.

Destin, fondly known as "The World's Luckiest Fishing Village," is a destination that enchants visitors with its natural beauty, vibrant culture, and endless opportunities for fun and exploration. Whether you're a first-time visitor or a seasoned traveler returning to your favorite spots, this guide is designed to enrich your experience and help you uncover the many layers of this stunning coastal gem.

In these pages, you'll find detailed insights and tips covering every aspect of your Destin journey. From thrilling water activities like deep-sea fishing and snorkeling to tranquil moments on secluded beaches, this book has something for everyone. We delve into the rich history of Destin, sharing stories of its humble beginnings and growth into a beloved vacation hotspot. We guide you through the best times to visit, ensuring you make the most of Destin's seasonal charms and local festivities.

This guide is not just about where to go and what to do, but also about how to connect with the spirit of Destin. We've curated recommendations for the finest dining experiences, from seafood shacks serving fresh catches to elegant restaurants with stunning views. Discover unique attractions, family-friendly activities, and tranquil spots perfect for mindfulness and relaxation.

I've also included practical advice to make your trip seamless, from packing essentials and transportation tips to safety guidelines and local customs. Our aim is to provide you with all the tools you need for an unforgettable vacation, one filled with memories you'll cherish long after the sun sets on your time in Destin.

So, grab your sunhat, slip on your flip-flops, and let the adventure begin.

INTRODUCTION

Welcome to Destin, a seaside paradise with green waters and pristine white dunes. Destin, located on Florida's Emerald Coast, provides incredible activities, breathtaking views, hidden gems, and ultimate relaxation. Destin has something for everyone, whether you want to catch a fish, relax on the beach, or experience local culture.

Imagine waking up to the sound of gentle waves lapping the coast, the perfume of salt air invigorating your senses, and the prospect of a day spent in the sun, sea, and sand. Consider seeing colorful marketplaces, eating excellent seafood at charming beachside restaurants, and learning about Destin's rich history and vibrant culture.

Our guide is aimed to help you discover the best of Destin. We've got you covered for large aquatic adventures and must-see attractions, as well as hidden gems off the main road and peaceful spots for relaxing. We'll show you the best sites, restaurants, calm escapes, and local secrets to make your trip special.

Pack your luggage, grab your sunscreen, and get ready to discover Destin's enchantment. Whether you are a first-time visitor or returning to relive your fondest moments, this book will be your trusted companion, transporting you to the heart of Destin's attraction. Welcome to Destin, where adventure and entertainment await you!

Overview of Destin

Destin, on Florida's Emerald Coast, is a jewel of a resort noted for its stunning white sand beaches, emerald-green oceans, and vibrant, welcoming town. Destin, named the "World's Luckiest Fishing Village," offers a terrific mix of outdoor activities, excellent restaurants, and rich cultural events. From the bustling Destin Harbor Boardwalk to the serene dunes of Henderson Beach State Park, there's something for everyone. Destin provides an unforgettable vacation, whether you're seeking adrenaline-pumping water sports, peaceful nature treks, or simply a relaxing day in the sun.

History

Early days: Destin, Florida, has a long history, beginning with the rich traditions of indigenous peoples and progressing to become a well-known fishing town. The region, known for its stunning emerald-green lakes and sugar-white sand beaches, was once home to Native American tribes such as the Creek and Seminole. These tribes relied on the abundant natural resources, particularly the large fishing regions.

The region was initially visited by Europeans in the early 16th century, specifically Spanish adventurers. Notable among them was Juan Ponce de León, who is supposed to have traveled through the area in 1513 in search of the legendary Fountain of Youth. However, it wasn't until the 17th century that more detailed records of the region became available, mostly from Spanish and subsequently French explorers who chartered the Gulf Coast.

Destin's current history began in the mid-nineteenth century with the arrival of Leonard Destin, a fisherman from New London, Connecticut. In 1845, Leonard Destin relocated to the area that today bears his name, laying the groundwork for what would become a thriving fishing village. Destin is widely credited for pioneering the local fishing industry, capitalizing on the Gulf of Mexico's abundant fish populations. Destin is regarded as "The World's Luckiest Fishing Village," to honor his legacy.

Development and Growth: The completion of the East Pass, a major maritime path, in the 1930s hastened Destin's rise. This technical marvel allowed larger fishing vessels to approach the port, enhancing the town's reputation as a fishing hub. Destin began to attract tourists in the mid-20th century, drawn by its picturesque beaches and excellent fishing opportunities.

In the 1970s and 1980s, the construction of Destin Harbor and the development of adjacent Okaloosa Island transformed the area into a major tourist destination. Resorts, hotels, and other facilities were built to accommodate the increasing number of visitors. During this time, several charter fishing companies formed, capitalizing on the town's maritime heritage.

Modern period

Today, Destin is a vibrant town that mixes its historical roots with modern amenities. The Destin Fishing Rodeo, inaugurated in 1948, is a popular annual event that draws anglers from all over the world. Harbor Walk Village is a busy shopping, dining, and entertainment destination that mixes historic charm with modern conveniences.

Despite its growth, Destin retains its small-town charm and strong ties to its fishing heritage. Destin's commitment to preserving the natural beauty and biological health of its beaches and oceans ensures that it remains a popular destination for future generations.

Cultural and Historical Preservation

Local groups such as the Destin Past & Fishing Museum help to preserve Destin's history. This museum offers a detailed look at Destin's history, with artifacts, photographs, and displays that illustrate the city's evolution from a small fishing village to a flourishing tourist attraction.

Destin's history is an intriguing blend of indigenous culture, European discovery, and American colonization. It is a transforming story driven by the sea's perennial appeal and the enterprising energy of its people. Destin's history, from its roots as a fishing town to its current status as a popular vacation destination, displays the enduring appeal of its natural beauty and the community's resilience.

Geography and Landscape

Emerald oceans and gorgeous beaches.

Destin, Florida, is noted for its unique topography and magnificent scenery, which includes emerald-green canals and sugar-white sandy beaches. The bright color of the Gulf of Mexico waters is owing to the region's high concentration of small plankton and clean quartz crystal sand, which reflect sunlight and give the sea its distinctive green tinge. The beaches, constructed of finely powdered quartz crystal from the Appalachian Mountains, are among the world's whitest and softest, offering a beautiful contrast to the clear waters.

Choctawhatchee Bay and East Pass

Destin's geographical location is further defined by the Choctawhatchee Bay to the north and the Gulf of Mexico to the south. Choctawhatchee Bay, a brackish water basin, supports a complex marine ecosystem and serves as an important nursery for numerous fish species. The bay's sheltered waters are ideal for boating, fishing, and other outdoor activities.

The East Pass, a man-made strait between the Gulf of Mexico and Choctawhatchee Bay, is a significant feature of Destin's geography. This navigational waterway was created in the 1930s and has since been maintained to benefit the local fishing industry and facilitate marine traffic. The East Pass is crucial to the bay's natural balance because it allows saltwater and freshwater to mix, sustaining a variety of marine species.

Coastal Dune Lakes

One of Destin's most distinguishing characteristics is the presence of coastal dune lakes. These peculiar geological traits are only found in a few locations around the world, including Northwest Florida, Madagascar, Australia, and New Zealand. Coastal dune lakes are freshwater lakes located among dunes and separated from the Gulf of Mexico by a tiny stretch of beach. They frequently exchange water with the Gulf, creating a dynamic environment that supports a wide variety of plant and animal species. Camp Creek Lake and Morris Lake are two lakes in Destin that offer opportunities for kayaking, bird watching, and nature photography.

Henderson Beach State Park

Henderson Beach State Park is a prime example of Destin's preserved natural beauty. This protected area includes about a mile of natural shoreline with towering dunes, coastal scrub flora, and a diverse array of wildlife. The park provides a glimpse of the region's native ecosystems, which have largely remained undisturbed by urbanization. Visitors can enjoy hiking trails, picnics, and camping while admiring the tranquility and natural beauty of Destin's oceanfront.

The Okaloosa Island and Destin Harbor

The terrain of Destin is further impacted by Okaloosa Island to the west and Destin Harbor to the south. Okaloosa Island is a barrier island with extra-white sand beaches and recreational activities. It serves as a barrier against storms and tidal surges, protecting the mainland and contributing to the area's unique coastal landscape.

Destin Harbor, the city's focal point, serves as both a historical and functional landmark. It features a thriving marina, where charter fishing boats, pleasure yachts, and tour boats dock. The port area is a bustling hub of activity, with restaurants, shopping, and entertainment opportunities for both residents and visitors. The harbor's infrastructure has been built to blend in with the surrounding nature, preserving the beauty of Destin's coastline.

Wildlife & Conservation

Destin's unusual geography also supports a diverse array of animals. The coastal waters are home to dolphins, sea turtles, and a variety of fish species, making it an excellent location for wildlife viewing and fishing. Birdwatchers can see a variety of species, including herons, egrets, and ospreys, particularly near coastal dune lakes and protected parklands.

Destin's conservation initiatives are aimed at maintaining a delicate balance between the development and preservation of natural resources. Organizations and local governments work tirelessly to protect Destin's beaches, dune systems, and marine habitats from pollution and overdevelopment so that future generations can enjoy the same natural beauty that defines it now.

Finally, Destin's unusual geology and terrain are characterized by gorgeous beaches, vibrant waterways, rare coastal dune lakes, and diversified ecosystems. Destin's commitment to conservation and sustainable development ensures that its natural beauty and biological health are preserved, making it a popular destination for nature lovers and outdoor enthusiasts alike.

How To Use This Guide

Welcome to your ideal companion for exploring Destin This book is intended to be your go-to reference, whether you're organizing a trip from scratch or looking to optimize an existing itinerary. Here's how to make the best of it.

Discover Epic Adventures: To discover the best activities in Destin, start with our Epic Adventures chapter. Discover the best way to fuel your adventurous spirit, from thrilling water sports to quiet nature hikes.

Plan Your Must-See Sights: Visit the Must-See Sights area to ensure you don't miss any of Destin's well-known or scenic attractions. This section of the book discusses anything from historical landmarks to magnificent vistas.

Discover Hidden Gems: For those who enjoy getting off the beaten path, our Hidden Gems area features lesser-known landmarks and secret locales that only locals are aware of.

Relax and rejuvenate: Do you want to unwind? Check out Relaxation & Wellness for the best spas, beautiful beaches, and tranquil parks to revitalize.

Family Fun: Are you traveling with children? Our Family Fun area is packed with activities and attractions to keep the whole family entertained and happy.

Savor Local Flavors: The Dining and Nightlife chapter will guide you to the best restaurants and vibrant nightlife districts, allowing you to truly experience the local cuisine and culture.

Shop 'Till You Drop: Finally, go to the Shopping chapter to find the best shopping locations, unusual boutiques, and local markets for souvenirs, and more.

Insider tips, practical advice, and detailed maps are included throughout the guide to help you navigate and make the most of your visit. Whether you're traveling for a weekend or staying for an extended period, this guide will help you have a great holiday in Destin. Welcome to your adventure!

Getting There

Destin is a location that is both easily accessible and well-connected, making travel as enjoyable as the stay. Here's how to get to Destin via air, vehicle, or boat.

By Air: Flying to Destin is simple, with multiple local airports providing convenient options for travelers:

The nearest airport is Destin-Fort Walton Beach Airport (VPS), which is only 16 miles from Destin. VPS has multiple flights from key cities across the United States and is served by a variety of airlines, including American Airlines, Delta, and Southwest. To travel to your destination from the airport, you can easily rent a car, take a taxi, or a shuttle service.

Northwest Florida Beaches International Airport (ECP): Located around 50 miles away in Panama City Beach, ECP is another excellent option for flights from various national hubs. Rental cars, taxis, and shuttle services are available to get you to Destin.

Pensacola International Airport (PNS): Located 70 miles west of Destin, PNS offers a wider range of flight options.

It takes a little longer, but the trip down the coast is gorgeous and enjoyable. Rental cars and shuttle services are also available.

By Road: Traveling to Destin by car is a flexible and appealing option. This is what you should know.

Interstate 10 (I-10): This significant east-west highway runs through the Florida Panhandle, making it a convenient route from other parts of Florida, Alabama, or elsewhere. Take the proper exit towards Destin and travel along the local roads, admiring the beauty.

U.S. Route 98: This beachside route is Destin's main thoroughfare. It is well-connected and simple to use, and it will take you directly to Destin's center. Be alert during peak travel hours, since traffic can be heavy, especially during the summer months.

Beautiful Routes: If you have time, drive one of the scenic byways, such as 30A, which offers stunning views of the coastline and little coastal communities.

By The Sea: For those who prefer to sail, arriving by boat is an excellent way to discover Destin.

Destin Harbor is a popular boating destination, with several marinas and docking facilities available. Whether you arrive by private yacht or lease a boat, the harbor provides easy access to the city and its amenities.

Baytowne Marina: Located within the Sandestin Golf and Beach Resort, this marina is another excellent choice for boaters. It offers full-service amenities and is conveniently positioned near Destin's major attractions.

For those sailing the Intracoastal Waterway, connecting to Choctawhatchee Bay will take you right to Destin. This technique is ideal for viewing the region's natural splendor and quiet oceans.

Getting to Destin is part of the journey, no matter how you get there. With easy transportation options by air, land, and sea, you'll be well on your way to experiencing everything this Emerald Coast treasure has to offer. Safe travels.

When Should You Visit?

When planning a trip to Destin, consider the best time to enjoy everything this beautiful beach town has to offer. To help you plan your visit, here's a summary of the seasonal weather, the optimum times for specific activities, and a calendar of local festivals and events.

Seasonal Weather Overview

Destin has a pleasant subtropical climate, making it suitable for year-round visits. Nonetheless, each season offers a unique experience.

Spring (March-May) is one of the best times to visit Destin. Temperatures range from the mid-60s to mid-80s°F (18-29°C). The weather is nice but not scorching, and the water is perfect for swimming and other aquatic activities. Spring break attracts large crowds, but it also generates a lively atmosphere.

Destin's peak tourist season is from June to August, with temperatures ranging from the mid-70s to low 90s°F (24-34°C). Expect a greater crowd and higher prices. This is a great time for beach activities, boating, and fishing. Make sure to book your accommodations and activities well in advance.

Fall (September to November) offers a more relaxed atmosphere, with temperatures ranging from the mid-60s to the mid-80s°F (18-29°C). The weather is pleasant, and the water is still safe for swimming. Fall is also hurricane season, so keep an eye on the forecast.

The quietest season in Destin is winter (December-February), when temperatures range from the mid-40s to mid-60s°F (7-20°C). While the temperature is too chilly to swim, this season is great for exploring nature trails, trying local cuisine, and participating in holiday events. It's also an excellent time to find great deals on lodging.

Best times for activities

Swimming, snorkeling, paddleboarding, and other water activities are best enjoyed between late spring and early fall. The sea is warm, and the days are long and clear.

Destin's reputation as the "World's Luckiest Fishing Village" assures that fishing is excellent all year long. However, the best months are from April to November, when there are numerous fishing competitions and the peak season for various species.

Golf is best played during the colder months of spring and fall. The courses are less crowded, and the weather is warm and pleasant.

Trekking and Nature Walks: Fall and winter are wonderful seasons for trekking and exploring nature trails. The weather is colder, and the landscapes are vibrant with seasonal colors.

Local Festivities and Events

Destin has various festivals and events throughout the year to provide a cultural and festive touch to your visit:

Destin Seafood Festival (October): This famous annual event commemorates Destin's rich fishing heritage. Destin Harbor offers great seafood, live music, and family-friendly activities.

Destin Fishing Rodeo (October): This month-long fishing contest attracts anglers from all around the world. The

Destin Harbor Boardwalk boasts excellent catches and frequent weigh-ins.

Billy Bowlegs Pirate Festival (June): A fun event featuring pirate-themed parades, fireworks, and celebrations. It's a family-friendly festival that reflects Destin's bold personality.

The Emerald Coast Blue Marlin Classic (June) is one of the region's most well-known fishing tournaments. It's a must-see event for fishing enthusiasts, with big prizes and huge catches.

Christmas Boat Procession (December): A joyful procession of beautifully decorated boats that illuminate the waterfront. It's a fantastic event that kicks off the holiday season in Destin.

You can plan a memorable visit to Destin by considering the seasonal weather, the best times for your favorite activities, and local festivals and events.

1. EPIC ADVENTURES

1.1 Water Activities

Welcome to Destin's Water Wonderland. Whether you're a seasoned water enthusiast or just starting, Destin provides a splash-tastic array of activities that will leave you exhilarated and wanting more. Destin's lush waterways are your ultimate playground, offering everything from the thrill of deep-sea fishing to the quiet delight of paddleboarding and kayaking.

Deep Sea Fishing

Are you ready to embark on an amazing deep-sea fishing adventure? Destin, known as the "World's Luckiest Fishing Village," is an excellent spot for capturing big fish. Imagine the exhilaration of battling a massive marlin or a savage snapper while the blue Gulf seas stretch out in front of you.

Book a boat with an experienced local skipper who knows the best fishing spots. They will provide you with all of the essential equipment, bait, and advice. Whether you're a novice or an expert, they'll make sure you have a fantastic day on the lake.

Best Time to Go: While you can fish all year, the peak season runs from April to November. This is when the seas are teeming with various fish species.

Remember to pack sunscreen, a hat, and a cooler for your catch of the day. Remember to bring your camera; you'll want to capture the moment you catch your prize fish!

Snorkeling and Scuba Diving

Dive into Destin's fascinating undersea realm, where you'll find abundant marine life and crystal-clear waters. Whether you're snorkeling in small reefs or scuba diving in deeper waters, your aquatic adventure will be spectacular.

Snorkeling Spots: Norriego Point has calm, shallow waters perfect for snorkeling. The East Jetty, near Destin's harbor, is another excellent area to swim with colorful fish and unusual marine life.

Scuba Diving Sites: For scuba enthusiasts, the Destin Jetties and sunken ships of the constructed reefs offer thrilling underwater exploring. Certified divers can take guided tours to discover hidden gems beneath the surface.

Gear and Safety: Rent high-quality equipment from local stores or join a guided tour that includes all you need. Safety is crucial, therefore always snorkel or dive with a buddy and follow local rules.

Paddleboarding and Kayaking

On a paddleboard or kayak, you may see Destin's calm beauty from a different perspective. This tranquil yet thrilling activity allows you to glide around quiet bays, explore secret coves, and get close to nature.

Paddleboarding: Stand-up paddleboarding (SUP) is a great way to enjoy the water while getting some workout. Beginners can take lessons to get started, while experienced paddlers can explore stunning locations like Choctawhatchee Bay.

Kayaking: Rent a kayak and paddle around the tranquil waters of Henderson Beach State Park or Choctawhatchee Bay. Kayaking is perfect for observing wildlife and savoring the stunning coastal scenery.

What to Bring: Wear comfortable swimwear, water shoes, and a waterproof bag for storing your belongings. Don't forget to hydrate and apply sunscreen before leaving.

Are you prepared to create a splash? These water activities in Destin provide limitless entertainment and adventure for everyone.

- **On the Waves**

Prepare to ride the waves and feel the salty wind on your face because Destin's waters are calling! Whether you're a speed demon, a thrill-seeker, or simply enjoy the open sea, Destin has the perfect wave-riding activity for you. Let's explore the world of boat rentals, jet skiing, and parasailing; trust us, you'll have a great time.

Boat Rentals and Sailing

Hello, future captains! Do you want to spend the day on the water at your own pace? Renting a boat in Destin means creating your own floating paradise. If you wish to sail, fish, or simply rest in the sun, there is a boat for you.

Boat Rentals: Destin's boat rental companies provide anything from sleek speedboats to huge pontoon boats. Gather your crew, pack a meal, and set sail for an unforgettable day. Imagine exploring hidden coves, mooring at Crab Island, and possibly seeing dolphins!

Sailing Adventures: Do you prefer to have someone else navigate? Join a sailing adventure and feel the breeze in your sails as you glide around the emerald lakes.

Experienced captains will lead you on a leisurely excursion, sharing local anecdotes and providing the best views.

Pack sunscreen, sunglasses, and a playlist of your favorite songs. Also, if you are prone to seasickness, bring some ginger candies or motion sickness bands; nobody wants to chum the seas!

Jet Skiing

Ready to pump up the excitement? Jet skiing in Destin is like having your own personal water rollercoaster. Hold on tight, for this voyage will be fast, furious, and incredibly entertaining!

Zoom Around: Rent a jet ski and experience the exhilaration of racing across the ocean at high speeds. Whether you're a seasoned surfer or a newbie, the sensation of skimming the waves is pure adrenaline.

Explore: Join a guided jet ski expedition to find hidden treasures, learn about local wildlife, and even outperform your friends. It's a high-energy way to explore more of Destin's stunning coastline.

Safety first: Always wear a life jacket and pay attention to the safety instructions. Remember that jet skis don't have brakes, so practice your spins and keep an eye out for nearby boats. Oh, and don't fall off unless you're going for a nice dip!

Parasailing

Have you ever had a dream about flying? Parasailing in Destin can make you feel like a superhero soaring through the sky. Prepare for an unforgettable bird's-eye view of the gorgeous coastline!

Strap into your harness and prepare to fly. As the boat speeds, you will gradually rise into the air. Before you know it, you're floating far over the lake, appreciating the amazing panoramic view below.

View It All: From your lofty perch, you can see for miles, including the magnificent emerald oceans, bustling harbor, and possibly some sea turtles or dolphins swimming beneath. It's a distinct viewpoint.

Pro tip: Dress comfortably and secure your eyewear. Most importantly, relax and enjoy the journey. If you're feeling daring, ask for a "dip" - a gentle plunge into the water followed by a return to the surface. Just don't forget to scream in delight (or fright); it's all part of the experience!

Destin's Waves is excited to take you on an amazing tour. You'll have a terrific time whether you're driving your boat, jet skiing like an expert or parasailing. So put on your life jacket, grab your sense of adventure, and let's make some waves!

- **Exploring the coast**

Destin's shoreline is a treasure trove of natural beauty and exciting experiences waiting to be found. Imagine drifting over emerald-green waves, feeling the sun on your face, and discovering the hidden gems that distinguish Destin. Whether you want to meet playful dolphins, take a relaxing harbor tour, or hop from one island paradise to the next, we have you covered. Let's set sail and explore!

Dolphin Tours

Prepare for a delightful encounter with one of the ocean's friendly creatures! Dolphin excursions in Destin are a must-do, giving an unforgettable experience that will make you smile from ear to ear.

Meet the Dolphins: Board a comfortable boat and sail out to the dolphin hotspots. Keep a lookout for bottlenose dolphins with their unique fins and happy leaps as you glide over the brilliant water. These curious and cunning animals frequently swim right up to the boats, putting on a show that you will never forget.

Most dolphin tours last about two hours, giving you plenty of time to see dolphins and explore the stunning shoreline scenery. Knowledgeable guides share fascinating information about these remarkable creatures and their marine home.

Bring your camera for some incredible photo possibilities, and don't forget your sunscreen and hat. Dolphins are most active in the early morning and late afternoon, so plan your trip around those times for the best experience.

Harbor Cruises

A harbor tour is a more leisurely but equally interesting way to experience the sights and sounds of Destin's bustling waterfront.

Cruise and Relax: Board a comfortable boat for a scenic cruise of Destin Harbor. Harbor excursions are great for unwinding while taking in the breathtaking views of the marina, opulent waterfront residences, and lively promenades.

Sunset Magic: Book an evening cruise to see the breathtaking beauty of a Destin sunset. As the sun sets below the horizon, the skylights in vibrant hues of orange, pink, and purple, create a stunning backdrop for your journey.

Pro tip: Bring a light jacket for the brisk nighttime wind and your favorite wine to celebrate the breathtaking views. Some cruises offer supper or beverages on board, making for a truly unforgettable experience.

Island Hopping (Crab Island and Beyond)

If you appreciate adventure and exploration, island hopping in Destin is a blast. From well-known Crab Island to hidden gems, there's a bit of bliss waiting for you.

Crab Island: This underwater sandbar has become one of Destin's most popular attractions. Rent a boat or take a tour to Crab Island, where you may wander through the shallow, crystal-clear waters, join floating parties, or simply rest and enjoy the sun. cuisine boats and floating bars enhance the experience by serving delicious cuisine and refreshing beverages.

Beyond Crab Island: Venture further to discover lesser-known islands and secluded beaches. Norriego Point and Jolee Island offer peaceful retreats where you can dine, swim, and explore at your leisure.

Pro tip: To explore the underwater splendor, bring a cooler with food and beverages, water shoes, and snorkeling gear. If you prefer a more serene experience, come during the week or early in the morning.

Exploring Destin's coastline is an exciting and memorable experience. From dolphin encounters to harbor cruises to island hopping, each activity offers a unique opportunity to see the Emerald Coast's natural beauty and vibrant life.

1.2 Land-based Thrills

Destin's allure extends beyond its shimmering waves; its beautiful scenery and active outdoor activities offer endless opportunities for thrill and adventure. Whether you're a nature lover, a golfer, or an adrenaline junkie, Destin's land-based activities will provide remarkable experiences. Let's zipline across the best hiking and nature paths, golf courses, and exciting adventure parks!

Hiking and Nature Trails

Lace up your hiking boots and prepare to explore Destin's stunning nature trails. These paths wind through stunning landscapes, offering a tranquil escape into nature as well as the opportunity to observe native flora and wildlife up close.

Henderson Beach State Park is a spectacular nature trail that takes you across coastal dune habitats. The course is simple to follow and suitable for families. As you walk, take in the sights and sounds of the local wildlife, and don't forget to stop at the beautiful overlooks for breathtaking views of the Gulf.

Fred Gannon Rocky Bayou State Park offers a variety of trails that wind through pine trees and along the bayou. The Rocky Bayou Trail is popular, having a mix of shady paths and open fields where you can watch deer, birds, and other creatures.

The Timpoochee Trail, which runs 18.6 miles along Scenic Highway 30A, provides stunning views of coastal dunes, state parks, and picturesque seaside settlements.

Bring plenty of water, sunscreen, a hat, and a map or trail app. Hiking in the early morning or late afternoon is ideal for avoiding the midday heat and obtaining the best light for photographs.

Golf Courses

Destin is a golfer's dream, with a wide range of courses to suit all skill levels. Imagine teeing off against a backdrop of emerald green fairways and the shimmering Gulf; it's every golfer's fantasy!

Regatta Bay Golf & Yacht Club: This award-winning course is known for its lush, scenic layout and challenging holes. The course passes through marshes and woodlands, offering breathtaking views and the opportunity to observe local wildlife.

Kelly Plantation Golf Club: Designed by Fred Couples, this course features immaculate greens, beautiful water views, and an inviting atmosphere. It's perfect for both serious golfers and those who want a more casual game.

Emerald Bay Golf Club: This course, situated on the banks of Choctawhatchee Bay, offers challenging holes with spectacular scenery. The well-kept greens and fairways provide a delightful golfing experience.

Make your tee appointments in advance, especially during peak seasons. Don't forget your sunscreen, hat, and plenty of beverages. Most courses provide rentals, but if you have specific club preferences, bring your own.

Adventure parks and zip-lining

Destin's adventure parks and zipline options are sure to get your heart rate soaring. These activities offer an amazing opportunity to experience the region's natural beauty from a variety of angles.

The Track Family Fun Park offers a variety of activities, including go-kart racing, mini-golf, and thrill rides.

The Sky Flyer attraction is a must-see since it allows you to experience freefall while remaining safely connected.

Baytowne Adventure Zone: Located in the heart of the Village of Baytowne Wharf, this adventure zone features a zipline that takes you over the lagoon. A ropes course, climbing tower, and eurobungy offer enjoyment for individuals of all ages.

Zipline at HarborWalk Village: Experience the thrill of zipping over the bustling HarborWalk Village. This zipline offers stunning views of the port and Gulf, combining adventure with a scenic setting.

Dress comfortably and adequately for the weather, and wear closed-toe footwear. Check the height and weight limitations for zip lines and other rides. Arrive early to avoid long waits, especially on weekends and holidays.

From calm hikes and picturesque golf courses to adrenaline-pumping adventure parks, Destin's land-based attractions provide something for everyone. So get your gear, assemble your friends or family, and prepare to have a great time in Destin's beautiful surroundings!

2. MUST-SEE SIGHTS

2.1 Beaches and Parks

Destin's beaches and parks, where sun-kissed sands meet the Gulf's magnificent waves, make every moment feel like a postcard-perfect memory waiting to happen. From the serene serenity of Henderson Beach State Park to the lively atmosphere of James Lee Park and the lovely allure of Crystal Beach, each location offers a taste of heaven. Let us delve in and discover the wonders that await.

- **Henderson Beach State Park:** Welcome to Henderson Beach State Park, a serene retreat where the concerns of the world are washed away with each gentle wave. Imagine walking down the beautiful shoreline, your toes sinking into smooth, powder-white sand and the emerald-green waters beckoning you to dip them. The park's coastal dune ecology is breathtaking, teeming with natural flora and wildlife that add to the magical atmosphere.

Escape to nature: Wander along the park's natural pathways, shaded by towering pines and swaying palms, and immerse yourself in the beauty of pristine wilderness.

Beach Bliss: Spread out your beach blanket, grab a good book, and allow the rhythmic sound of the waves to transport you to a state of delightful relaxation.

Family Fun: Bring a picnic and spend the day making memories with loved ones by building sandcastles, playing beach volleyball, or simply relaxing under the warm Florida sun.

Arrive early to ensure your space, especially during peak seasons. Bring plenty of sunscreen, water, and snacks, and don't forget to greet the friendly park rangers, who are usually willing to provide insider tips and experiences.

- **James Lee Park:** Calling all beachgoers and sun worshippers: James Lee Park is the perfect playground! This vibrant beach area, located along the scenic Highway 98, is a favorite hangout for both locals and visitors. With its long sandy beach, crystal-clear oceans, and active setting, it's the perfect place to relax and let your problems go.

Beachside Bliss: Grab your beach chair and umbrella and stake your claim on the sand, where you can spend the day basking in the sun's warm rays and cooling off with refreshing dives in the Gulf.

Water Adventures: Feeling adventurous? Rent a paddleboard or kayak to explore the sparkling waters at your leisure, or try your hand at jet skiing for a thrilling experience.

Beachside Eats: When hunger strikes, head to one of the nearby beachfront restaurants for a taste of fresh seafood or a refreshing tropical drink; nothing says vacation like dining with your toes in the sand.

Bring towels, sunscreen, and plenty of water with you to the beach. If you're feeling daring, challenge your friends to a sandcastle-building competition; the loser gets ice cream!

Crystal Beach: Welcome to Crystal Beach, a charming seaside community where the relaxed vibe and warm smiles will make you feel right at home. This beloved neighborhood beach is a hidden gem waiting to be discovered, with sugar-white beaches, blue waters, and picture-perfect sunsets that turn the sky pink and gold.

Beachfront Bliss: Kick off your shoes and feel the silky sand between your toes as you take a stroll along the beach, collecting seashells and making memories that last a lifetime.

Sunset Serenade: As the day comes to an end, choose a comfortable spot on the beach and watch in awe as the sun sinks below the horizon, casting a warm light over the sea and creating a postcard-perfect scene.

Local Flavor: After a day of sun and surf, stop by the nearby shops and cafés for a scoop of homemade ice cream or to seek unique presents to remember your stay in paradise.

Embrace the local vibe by welcoming other beachgoers, striking up a conversation with a friendly local, and letting your inner child play.

Destin's beaches and parks offer limitless opportunities for recreation, adventure, and one-of-a-kind experiences, from the tranquil beauty of Henderson Beach State Park to the lively shoreline of James Lee Park and the charming allure of Crystal Beach. So grab your sunscreen, pack your sense of wonder, and get ready to have a lifetime of unforgettable experiences.

2.2 Historic and Cultural Sites

Welcome, adventurers, on a journey through Destin's vibrant history and cultural heritage. As you stroll through the time corridors, you will be captivated by the stories of persistence, ingenuity, and community spirit that have defined this beloved beach town. The fascinating exhibits at the Destin History & Fishing Museum, the ancient treasures at the Indian Temple Mound Museum, and the nostalgic beauty of the Camp Walton Schoolhouse Museum all offer an insight into Destin's history and culture. Let's go on this exciting journey together!

- **Destin History and Fishing Museum**

Step back in time as you wander through the historic corridors of the Destin History & Fishing Museum, where the sea breeze conveys echoes of a bygone era. This museum, located in the heart of Destin's historic port district, honors the town's rich fishing heritage while also remembering the lives of the brave men and women who built this city from the sea.

Exhibits Galore: Discover a treasure trove of antiques, photographs, and memorabilia that record Destin's evolution from a little fishing village to a thriving tourist destination. Each exhibit, which ranges from old fishing gear and boats to personal stories of local fishermen, offers a glimpse into the lives and livelihoods of those who lived on these waters.

Step aboard a model fishing vessel and try throwing a net or pulling in a large haul to immerse yourself in the sights, sounds, and fragrances of Destin's bustling docks. Interactive exhibits and multimedia displays clearly show the history of fishing, providing a fun and educational experience for guests of all ages.

Local Lore: Talk to experienced museum staff and volunteers who are eager to discuss the stories behind the exhibits. From legendary tales of spectacular fishing adventures to heartfelt anecdotes of community cooperation, their insights will deepen your respect for Destin's marine heritage.

Pro Tip: Take your time visiting each exhibit and don't be hesitant to ask questions; the museum staff will gladly share their knowledge and enthusiasm with you. Check the museum's program schedule for one-of-a-kind exhibitions, guest lecturers, and hands-on workshops that will help you learn more about Destin's history and culture.

They are currently open Tuesday through Saturday from 10:00 a.m. to 4:00 p.m. It's always a good idea to double-check their hours before you come by calling (850) 837-6610 or visiting their website.

- **Indian Temple Mound Museum**

When you visit the Indian Temple Mound Museum, expect to be transported back in time to a world of mystery and enchantment. Nestled among the lush flora of Fort Walton Beach, this archeological marvel offers an amazing glimpse into the lives of the indigenous peoples who inhabited this region thousands of years ago.

Ancient Artifacts: Discover a fascinating collection of artifacts, ceramics, and tools that provide details about the daily lives, ceremonies, and beliefs of the Native American tribes that once thrived in the area. From intricately carved shell decorations to ceremonial masks and pottery vessels, each piece tells a story of survival and cultural creativity.

Majestic Mounds: Step outside to witness the landscape's towering earthen mounds, which are remnants of ancient ceremonial sites used for community gatherings, religious rites, and social events. Climb to the peak for panoramic views of the surrounding area and imagine the vibrant tapestry of life that once flourished there.

Educational Programs: The museum offers a variety of educational programs, guided tours, and hands-on activities to help you learn more about Native American history and culture. Whether you are a seasoned archeologist or a complete novice, there is something for everyone to discover and admire.

Visit the museum's gift shop, where you'll find a carefully chosen selection of books, crafts, and souvenirs inspired by Native American culture and traditions. Take advantage of the museum's outdoor picnic area and beautiful strolling routes for a relaxing break surrounded by nature's splendor.

The museum is open year-round, from Tuesday to Saturday, from 9:00 a.m. to 4:00 p.m. Similar to the Destin History & Fishing Museum, check their hours before visiting by calling (850) 837-1566 or visiting their website.

- **Camp Walton Schoolhouse Museum**

The Camp Walton Schoolhouse Museum brings visitors back in time. Located in the heart of downtown Fort Walton Beach, this meticulously restored one-room schoolhouse brings visitors back to a simpler time when education was the foundation of community life.

Historical Haven: Explore the schoolhouse's pleasant interiors, where antique desks, chalkboards, and textbooks evoke memories from the past. Trace the evolution of education in Northwest Florida by utilizing historical pictures, papers, and souvenirs from the school's rich past.

Living History: Costumed docents bring history to life via interactive demonstrations, role-playing exercises, and storytelling sessions, allowing you to see and hear what a typical school day was like in the late nineteenth and early twentieth centuries. From math classes to spelling bees, you'll discover the delights and challenges of studying in the past.

Community Connections: Learn how the Camp Walton Schoolhouse impacted the lives of generations of students and teachers who passed through its halls. Learn about the pioneering educators who dedicated their careers to developing young minds, as well as the long-lasting relationships created in the schoolyard. Listen to personal narratives and oral histories from local inhabitants to learn more about education's enormous impact on the fabric of communal life.

This lovely museum has slightly different opening hours. They are open Tuesdays and Thursdays from 10:00 a.m. to 2:00 p.m. Because it is a small museum, calling (850) 837-0242 to check on availability is very important.

Pro Tip: Take a moment to reflect on how far education has come since the days of the one-room schoolhouse, and analyze the timeless principles of curiosity, perseverance, and lifelong learning that continue to define our lives today. Don't pass up the opportunity to participate in one of the museum's educational programs or historical reenactments, where you may personally experience history and make lasting memories with your family and friends.

Remember that these are average opening hours and may vary depending on the season or special events. To acquire the most up-to-date information, always check their websites or contact them directly.

The sounds of the past resonate through the historic halls of the Destin History & Fishing Museum, the Indian Temple Mound Museum, and the Camp Walton Schoolhouse Museum, revealing stories of bravery, ingenuity, and community spirit. As you immerse yourself in Destin's rich tapestry of history and culture, may you be inspired to treasure the legacy that binds us together and pave your path to a brighter future.

2.3 Scenic Locations

- **Destin Harbor Boardwalk**

Hello, explorers. Prepare for an exciting and discovery-filled journey as we set sail for Destin's vibrant heart, the renowned Harbor Boardwalk. Nestled among the Gulf Coast's dazzling waves, this vibrant promenade entices with promises of one-of-a-kind adventures, delectable cuisine, and boundless fun. Are you ready to explore? Let's dive in.

Scenic landscapes and coastal ambiance provide a sensory feast.

As you enter the Harbor Boardwalk, you'll be greeted by a breathtaking panorama. Every turn will reveal breathtaking vistas of the emerald-green rivers, teeming with colorful boats and bordered by swaying palm trees. The salty air transmits the flavor of the sea as well as other passengers' laughing, creating an energetic and inviting setting.

Sensory Delights: As you walk along the boardwalk, take in the sights, sounds, and fragrances of the Gulf Coast.

Every moment is a sensory delight, from the rhythmic lapping of the waves on the beach to the bright colors of sunset casting a golden glow.

Coastal Charm: Take in the boardwalk's tiny shops, beautiful cafes, and colorful street performers. Discover unique treasures, savor fresh seafood specialties, and enjoy the laid-back vibe of seaside living.

Bring your camera to capture those Instagram-worthy moments, and don't forget to wear sunscreen and sunglasses to stay safe while basking in the sun. Consider going during sunset or dawn for an extra dose of enchantment!

Exciting Activities and Thrilling Excursions

Are you prepared for some high-seas excitement? The Harbor Boardwalk serves as the starting point for a wide range of interesting water activities. Whether you're a thrill-seeker seeking a jet ski adventure or a leisurely cruiser wanting to see dolphins, there's something for everyone.

Aquatic Adventures: Put on your life jacket and prepare to ride the waves on a jet ski or paddleboard rental. Feel the wind in your hair and the sea spray on your skin as you glide over the Gulf, appreciating the panoramic views of Destin's coastline.

Dolphin Encounters: Join a guided dolphin cruise and set sail in search of these vibrant marine mammals. Keep an eye out for dorsal fins breaking the surface, and observe the beauty and grandeur of these incredible creatures as they play in their natural environment.

Schedule your water activities ahead of time to ensure availability, especially during peak seasons. Stay hydrated and reapply sunscreen frequently to protect your skin from the sun's rays. Most importantly, remember to have fun; these memories will last a lifetime!

Unforgettable Nights: Dining and Entertainment

As the sun goes down, the Harbor Boardwalk becomes a lively hub of nightlife and entertainment. From scrumptious seafood feasts to live music performances under the stars, the evening provides numerous chances for amusement and relaxation.

Culinary Delights: Enjoy a seafood feast at one of the boardwalk's many waterfront restaurants. From delectable shrimp and crab legs to freshly caught fish cooked to perfection, the flavors of the Gulf will thrill your taste buds.

Relax on an outside terrace or at a coastal pub while outstanding artists perform live music. From laid-back acoustic melodies to frenetic dance numbers, there's something for everyone's musical preferences.

Make dinner reservations ahead of time, especially if you're visiting a popular restaurant or during peak hours.

After dinner, consider taking a walk along the boardwalk to take in the sights and sounds of the night.

Norriego Point

Welcome to Norriego Point, where nature's beauty meets the allure of adventure on the beaches of Destin. This stunning parcel of land, nestled at the mouth of the East Pass, is a hidden gem just waiting to be discovered. Norriego Point, with its sun-kissed beaches and crystal-clear oceans teeming with marine life, is a paradise for outdoor enthusiasts and environmentalists alike. Let us embark on a journey to experience the beauty of this beach paradise!

Coastal Splendor: Sun, Sand, and Sea

As you approach Norriego Point, prepare to be swept away by the overpowering majesty of your surroundings. The smooth, powdery sands stretch for kilometers, beckoning you to dip your toes into the warmth and experience the gentle caress of the Gulf breeze. The crystal-clear seas lap against the coast, glittering in shades of emerald and turquoise, tempting you to dive in and explore.

Beachside Bliss: Find the perfect spot on the sand to soak in the sun's rays while listening to the soothing beat of the waves. Whether you're relaxing with a good book or building sandcastles with your family, every moment spent at Norriego Point is pure joy.

Shoreline Strolls: Take a walk down the beach and let your problems wash away with the tide. Keep an eye out for gorgeous seashells and sand dollars washed ashore, since these are treasures waiting to be discovered by alert beachgoers.

Pack a picnic lunch and plenty of water to stay hydrated on your beach day. Don't forget to bring sunscreen and a beach umbrella for extra sun protection, and leave only footprints while exploring this pure natural treasure.

Aquatic Adventures: Explore the Waters.

Explore beyond the beach at Norriego Point and immerse yourself in an underwater world full of treasures. Whether you're a seasoned snorkeler or a beginner, the stunning waters surrounding the point offer endless opportunities for exploration and discovery.

Snorkeling Excursions: Put on your snorkel gear and prepare to be amazed by the vibrant underwater world that exists beneath the surface. Norriego Point is a snorkeler's dream because of its crystal-clear waters and abundance of marine life, which includes colorful fish, curious sea turtles, and the occasional dolphin.

Kayak and Paddleboard Rentals: Explore the tranquil waters surrounding Norriego Point by kayak or paddleboard. Paddle around the beach, explore hidden coves and inlets, and appreciate the natural beauty of this coastal sanctuary from a new perspective.

Pro Tip: Rent snorkeling gear and boats from reputable local operators to ensure safety and quality. Keep an eye on the weather and tidal currents, and always use a personal flotation device when at sea.

Conservation and Preservation: Protecting Norriego Point

While enjoying Norriego Point's natural beauty, keep in mind that this unique ecosystem is endangered and must be protected. Join local conservation efforts to help preserve the delicate balance of flora and fauna that inhabits this beach retreat.

Leave No Trace: Follow proper outdoor ethics and leave Norriego Point in the same condition you found it: clean, pristine, and litter-free. To ensure the long-term viability of this unique environment, proper waste disposal and wildlife habitat maintenance are required.

Educate and advocate: Raise awareness about the need for conservation and preservation efforts for Norriego Point and other natural areas. Encourage others to value the environment and take action to protect our planet for future generations to enjoy.

Help Norriego Point and the surrounding ecology by participating in beach cleanups and volunteering with local environmental organizations. Share your enthusiasm for the environment with others, inspiring a culture of conservation and sustainability.

As you say your goodbyes to Norriego Point, take a moment to enjoy the memories you've made and the beauty you've seen. Whether you spend the day lounging on the beach, snorkeling in the crystal-clear waters, or simply admiring the natural beauty of this coastal paradise, Norriego Point will always hold a particular place in your heart.

Jolee Island Nature Park

Jolee Island Nature Park combines natural rhythms with historical hints to create a contemplative haven. Tucked away in the heart of Destin, this hidden gem offers a calm escape from the hustle and bustle of everyday life. Jolee Island invites you on a journey of discovery and rejuvenation in the heart of Florida's Emerald Coast, complete with winding nature walks and tranquil lagoons teeming with wildlife.

Embrace serenity: Nature's playground.

As soon as you foot into Jolee Island, you'll feel a sense of calm wash over you. Towering oak trees provide shade from the sun, while native palms flow softly in the breeze, creating a lovely backdrop for your expedition. The island's twisting paths encourage exploration, leading you through lush forests, tranquil marshes, and hidden lagoons.

Trails of Tranquility: Put on your hiking boots and walk out on the island's network of nature trails, where each step brings you closer to the heart of the forest. Listen to the chorus of songbirds overhead as you travel through oak hammocks and pine woodlands, keeping a lookout for deer, raccoons, and other island wildlife.

Lakeside Bliss: Find a private spot along the tranquil beaches of the island's lagoons and unwind to the soothing sounds of nature. Whether you're enjoying a leisurely picnic with loved ones or simply reflecting by the water's edge, Jolee Island's calm beauty will uplift your spirits.

Pro Tip: Pack a picnic basket with your favorite foods and beverages to enjoy during your island trip. Keep your camera handy to capture the natural beauty that surrounds you, and wear comfortable shoes for exploring the island's pathways.

Discovering History: Tales of the Past

As you explore Jolee Island, you'll come across remnants of the past that shed light on the island's fascinating history. From ancient ruins to cultural artifacts, each discovery tells a story about the people who have lived on this island throughout time.

Historic Ruins: Explore the remnants of historic homesteads and houses that dot the island's surface, reflecting a bygone era when people made a living in the wilderness. These faded antiques are a reminder of the island's rich history and the fortitude of those who came before us.

Cultural Artifacts: Admire the artistically carved totem poles and sculptures that line the island's walkways, made by native artists to celebrate the island's natural beauty and cultural heritage. Each sculpture represents the creative practices and spiritual beliefs of the indigenous peoples that once inhabited these lands.

Take the time to grasp the historical significance of each relic and ruin you come across while touring Jolee Island.

Consider keeping a diary to capture your thoughts and observations as you reconnect with the island's past.

Land Stewardship is a key aspect of conservation and preservation.

As you enjoy the natural beauty of Jolee Island, remember the importance of conservation and preservation efforts to preserve this undisturbed wilderness for future generations to enjoy.

Responsible Exploration: When exploring the island, follow the Leave No Trace standards and tread carefully to respect the fragile mix of flora and fauna that live there. To decrease your environmental impact, properly dispose of rubbish and prevent disturbing wildlife.

Community Engagement: Take part in local conservation initiatives and volunteer opportunities to help preserve Jolee Island and other natural areas in the region. Working as a community, we can ensure that these vital resources are protected for years to come.

Educate yourself and others about the importance of conservation and preservation efforts, and advocate for legislation that promotes sustainable natural resource management. Lead by example and encourage others to become land stewards, so leaving an environmental legacy for future generations.

As you say goodbye to Jolee Island, take a moment to reflect on the memories you've made and the beauty you've witnessed. Jolee Island will always hold a particular place in your heart, whether you spend the day walking through the forest, discovering hidden historical treasures, or simply admiring nature's beauty. So, until next time, explorers, continue exploring, discovering, and appreciating the wonders of the world around you. Your new adventure awaits; embrace it with open arms and an open heart!

3. HIDDEN GEMS

3.1 Off the Beaten Path Beaches

Are you ready to escape the crowds and uncover the hidden beauties of Destin's coastline? Step off the beaten path and explore Eglin Beach Park, Princess Beach, and Okaloosa Island, three remote paradises waiting to be discovered. From pristine sands to turquoise waters, each of these off-the-beaten-path beaches offers its slice of coastal bliss. Let's dive in and discover the beauty that awaits!

- **Eglin Beach Park**

Eglin Beach Park, located along Choctawhatchee Bay's beaches, is a tranquil retreat away from the hustle and bustle of city life. As you walk down the meandering roads that lead to the water's edge, you'll observe how the stresses of everyday life drift away, replaced with a sense of quiet and tranquility.

Secluded Shoreline: Discover a stunning stretch of shoreline surrounded by swaying sea oats and dunes, offering a peaceful escape from the crowds. Whether you want to soak up the sun or enjoy a stroll along the water's edge, Eglin Beach Park is the perfect place to unwind and recharge.

Bayfront Beauty: Dip your toes into Choctawhatchee Bay's calm, shallow waters and let the stress melt away with each gentle wave. Pack a picnic and enjoy a seaside feast at one of the park's covered picnic tables, or simply unwind and soak up nature's beauty.

Bring binoculars to observe the unique wildlife of Eglin Beach Park, which includes lovely herons and majestic ospreys. Don't forget your camera to capture the breathtaking sunsets that color the sky pink and gold.

Princess Beach

Princess Beach, on the western outskirts of Destin, is a hidden gem that has yet to be discovered. With pure white sands and brilliant blue oceans, this secluded stretch of coastline is excellent for a day of sun, surf, and relaxation.

Untouched splendor: Sink your toes into the velvety sands of Princess Beach to witness nature's raw beauty, where development gives way to pristine dunes and natural flora. Whether you're basking in the sun or splashing in the surf, you'll feel a sense of liberation and escape unlike anywhere else.

Seaside Serenity: Find your private slice of heaven on Princess Beach and immerse yourself in the sights and sounds of the sea. Listen to the gentle lapping of the waves on the beach and feel the sun's warm embrace on your skin as you let go of your worries and anxiety.

Bring a beach umbrella and plenty of sunscreen to protect yourself from the sun's rays while spending the day at Princess Beach. Bring a set of snorkels to explore the underwater area teeming with marine life just offshore.

- **Okaloosa Island**

Okaloosa Island entices visitors with its beautiful beaches, crystal-clear waters, and many opportunities for adventure. This barrier island, only a short drive from Destin, offers a more relaxed option to its more well-known neighbors, with lots of space to spread out and soak in the sun.

Beachfront Bliss: Sink your toes into Okaloosa Island's sugar-white beaches and let your concerns wash away with the waves. Whether you're building sandcastles with the kids or having a romantic sunset stroll with your loved one, Okaloosa Island's beach is the perfect place to make memories.

Waterfront delights: Dive into the Gulf's peaceful, calming waters to discover a world of hidden underwater delights. Snorkel amid colorful fish and vibrant coral reefs, or go paddleboarding and kayaking for a thrilling day on the water.

Rent a beach chair and umbrella from a local vendor to make your day on Okaloosa Island more enjoyable. Bring a cooler with your favorite snacks and beverages to stay hydrated during the day.

As you say your goodbyes to Eglin Beach Park, Princess Beach, and Okaloosa Island, take a moment to reflect on the memories you've made and the beauty you've seen

3.2 Unique Attractions

Are you prepared to discover Destin's hidden gems? Destin offers a variety of interesting attractions, including lively farmers markets, charming beachside communities, and thrilling marine adventures. Join us on a journey of discovery as we explore the wide range of activities offered in this seaside paradise!

Destin Harbor Farmers Market

Prepare to have your taste buds tickled and your senses piqued at the Destin Harbor Farmers Market, a flourishing hub of local cuisine, handcrafted crafts, and community spirit. Nestled along the stunning coastline, this vibrant market celebrates the Gulf Coast's bountiful bounty and culinary culture. Let's embark on a delightful journey through the sights, smells, and flavors that await you at your favorite Destin destination!

Browse the booths packed with farm-fresh food, exquisite cheeses, and homemade delicacies to immerse yourself in a world of abundance. Every item at the Destin Harbor Farmers Market, from juicy heirloom tomatoes and crisp cucumbers to aromatic herbs and vibrant berries, reflects the region's fertile soil and dedication to sustainable agriculture.

Local Produce: Walk through rows of freshly picked fruits and vegetables to explore the Gulf Coast's vibrant colors and flavors. These seasonal delights, purchased directly from local farms and producers, are nutritious and flavorful, offering a true taste of the region's terroir.

Gourmet Treats: Indulge your taste buds with exquisite cheeses, handcrafted jams, freshly baked bread, and delectable pastries. Sample delectable dips and spreads, savor the sweetness of local honey, and stock up on pantry goods to elevate your culinary creations to new heights.

Arrive early to obtain the best selection of fresh produce and handcrafted items before they sell out. Bring a reusable tote bag to carry your purchases, and talk to the sellers - they're enthusiastic about their products and enjoy sharing tips and recipe ideas!

Community Connection: One of the highlights of the Destin Harbor Farmers Market is the opportunity to meet the passionate people behind the products. From farmers and artists to chefs and foodies, the market is a hive of creativity and friendship, where shared stories and meals foster a sense of belonging and community.

Meet the Farmers: Talk with the farmers and growers who care for the land, learn about their farming methods, and hear stories about their harvests. Learn about agriculture's seasonal cycles and the need to support local food systems for community and environmental health.

Artisanal Craftsmanship: Meet the artisans who put their hearts and souls into creating one-of-a-kind, handcrafted artifacts that embody the spirit of the Gulf Coast. Every piece, from pottery and jewelry to woodwork and textiles, tells a story about creativity, passion, and craftsmanship.

Take the time to talk to the merchants and other customers; you never know what culinary secrets or hidden gems you'll find! Consider taking a notepad to jot down cooking ideas and flavor combinations inspired by your market findings.

As you leave the Destin Harbor Farmers Market, you will take with you not only bags of fresh produce and artisanal goods but also a wealth of culinary inspiration and a greater connection to the vibrant community that keeps it running. Whether you're a seasoned chef or a novice home cook, the flavors and sensations you've tasted at the market are sure to inspire incredible culinary adventures in your kitchen.

Farm-Fresh Feasts: Let the seasonal richness of the market inspire your meal planning, creating meals that emphasize the flavors of the Gulf Coast in all their glory. Experiment with new ingredients and techniques, and let the local culinary scene's energy and creativity inspire your cuisine.

Sharing the Bounty: Gather friends and family around the table to enjoy the delicious bounty of your market haul. Whether you're hosting a casual brunch, a large dinner party, or a peaceful picnic by the sea, the delicacies at the Destin Harbor Farmers Market will delight and impress your visitors.

Keep an eye on the market's event calendar for cooking demos, tastings, and other special events that offer a unique opportunity to learn from local chefs and artisans. Don't be afraid to get creative in the kitchen; the best recipes are usually the product of spontaneity and imagination!

Village of Baytowne Wharf

Welcome to the Village of Baytowne Wharf, where coastal beauty meets casual luxury in the heart of Destin's waterfront district. This lively hamlet is a bustling hub of activity, with a diverse range of shops, restaurants, entertainment venues, and family-friendly attractions. Baytowne Wharf provides an unforgettable experience for individuals of all ages, whether they seek adventure, relaxation, or a taste of Gulf Coast friendliness. Let us explore the sights, sounds, and flavors that await you in this charming seaside enclave.

Wander the cobblestone streets of Baytowne Wharf, where exquisite boutiques and specialty businesses beckon with treasures to be found. From designer clothing and one-of-a-kind gifts to beachwear and souvenirs, the village offers a delightful shopping experience that captures the laid-back attitude of the Gulf Coast.

Boutique Finds: Choose from a carefully curated selection of fashion, accessories, and home décor items that represent the region's seaside lifestyle and creative spirit. Discover one-of-a-kind pieces that exude beach flair and add a bit of coastal charm to your wardrobe and home.

Visit the village's galleries and studios to support local artists and artisans, who create a diverse range of ceramics, jewelry, paintings, and sculptures inspired by the natural beauty of the Gulf Coast. Take home a piece of beach art to recall your time in paradise, or give it to a loved one as a treasured remembrance.

Take your time exploring the village's shops and galleries, uncovering hidden courtyards and picturesque roads along the way. Keep an eye out for special events and art festivals that showcase the talents of local artists while also offering one-of-a-kind purchasing experiences.

Family Fun and Adventure

Spend an adventure-filled day with the whole family at Baytowne Wharf, where excitement and entertainment are around every corner. The town offers visitors of all ages numerous opportunities for fun and adventure, such as thrilling attractions and outdoor activities, interactive experiences, and live entertainment.

Thrilling Rides: Ride the village's renowned carousel or soar to new heights on the BaytowneCed Zipline, which provides breathtaking views of the bay. Test your skills on the ropes course or challenge your friends to a round of mini-golf – the possibilities for amusement are endless!

Waterfront Wonders: Rent a paddleboat or kayak to explore Choctawhatchee Bay's tranquil waterways, or take a scenic cruise aboard the Solaris yacht for an unforgettable dining experience on the water. From sunset cruises to dolphin sightings, there's something for everyone at the Bay.

Buy a Baytowne Adventure Pass to gain cheap access to numerous attractions, allowing you to have more fun for less money. Check the village's event calendar for live music performances, festivals, and other special events happening during your stay.

Culinary Delights and Coastal Cuisine

Discover the flavors of the Gulf Coast at Baytowne Wharf's diverse array of restaurants, cafés, and diners, where culinary surprises await around every corner. From fresh seafood and Southern comfort food to foreign cuisine and inventive cocktails, the village offers a wonderful culinary experience for everyone.

Seafood Sensations: Savor the freshest seafood fished directly from the Gulf, with dishes ranging from classic shrimp and grits to creative sushi rolls and seafood boils. Dine al fresco on the beach or in a comfortable indoor setting; either way, you're in for a delicious feast.

Global Gastronomy: Explore the village's diverse dining scene, which includes everything from Italian trattorias and Mexican cantinas to Asian fusion eateries and French bistros. As you dine your way around Baytowne Wharf, you'll discover new flavors and relive old favorites.

Make dinner reservations ahead of time, especially during peak hours, or for riverfront seats with stunning views. Consider attending a culinary tour or food-tasting event to sample a variety of dishes while learning about the village's vibrant food culture.

Gulfarium – Marine Adventure Park

Dive into Marine Magic at Gulfarium Marine Adventure Park, where the wonders of the water are brought to life in an immersive and educational experience for the whole family. This famous attraction on Okaloosa Island lets guests get up close and personal with the fascinating animals that reside in the Gulf of Mexico. The Gulfarium promises a fascinating journey into the heart of the ocean, with happy dolphins and stunning sea lions among sleek sharks and colorful tropical species. Let's dive in and discover the underwater wonderland that awaits you.

Prepare to be amazed as you witness the extraordinary talents of the park's native marine animals in a range of thrilling performances and interactive encounters. From high-flying dolphin acrobatics to funny sea lion antics, each show highlights these extraordinary creatures' intelligence, agility, and natural habits.

Dolphin Presentations: Admire dolphins' elegance and beauty as they leap, spin, and splash their way through a variety of thrilling maneuvers. During instructive lectures led by the park's expert trainers, you will learn about these incredible marine species and their value to ocean ecosystems.

Sea Lion Shows: Be fascinated by sea lions' hilarious behaviors as they perform tricks, interact with their trainers, and demonstrate their extraordinary intelligence. Get up close and personal with these charming creatures during interactive feeding sessions and behind-the-scenes tours, which will help you understand their behavior and biology.

Arrive early to secure a prime viewing spot for the park's most popular acts, and think about upgrading to a VIP package for exclusive behind-the-scenes experiences and photo opportunities with the animals.

Interactive Exhibitions and Educational Experiences

Explore the park's interactive exhibits and educational displays to learn about the wonders of the aquatic world. Touch tanks and underwater viewing windows, as well as interactive feeding experiences and hands-on learning activities, will appeal to curious minds of all ages.

Touch Tanks: The park's touch tanks allow visitors to interact with a variety of aquatic species, including stingrays, horseshoe crabs, and sea stars. Experience the unique textures of these fascinating animals while learning about their adaptations and habitats from knowledgeable staff members.

Educational Programs: Learn more about marine life through educational programs and seminars led by the park's knowledgeable staff. Learn about the conservation challenges that marine ecosystems face, and how you can help protect the ocean and its inhabitants for future generations.

Take advantage of guided tours and interactive encounters provided by the park's professional personnel, who are eager to share their knowledge of marine life with visitors. During your visit, make sure to ask plenty of questions and take in as much information as possible.

Conservation and Environmental Stewardship

At Gulfarium Marine Adventure Park, conservation and environmental stewardship are integral to all we do. We are committed to protecting marine ecosystems and fostering sustainable practices that will keep the ocean healthy and vital for future generations via research, teaching, and activism.

Research Initiatives: Discover the park's current research and conservation efforts to better understand and protect marine biodiversity. Our scientists aim to increase our understanding of the ocean and its inhabitants, from observing dolphin behavior to calculating sea turtle populations.

Environmental Education: Our educational programs and outreach efforts aim to instill a love of nature and a sense of environmental responsibility. Through school field excursions, community events, and virtual learning opportunities, we hope to inspire individuals of all ages to become ocean stewards and conservation activists.

You may support the Gulfarium's conservation efforts by participating in donation campaigns, helping at beach cleanups, or joining the park's conservation club. Every small action helps to protect our planet's precious natural resources.

3.4 Best-Kept Secret Restaurants

Prepare your taste buds for a culinary journey unlike any other as we visit Destin's best-kept secret eateries, hidden gems buried away from the tourist crowds and waiting to be discovered by adventurous food lovers like you. These hidden culinary jewels, which range from modest bistros serving imaginative food to coastal eateries with breathtaking vistas and unique flavors, ensure a delicious and unforgettable eating experience. Let's go on a gastronomic excursion around Destin's culinary environment to discover the hidden gems that await!

Discover Destin's hidden culinary treasures, where fresh seafood, locally sourced ingredients, and innovative cooking techniques mix to create unforgettable dining experiences. These hidden gems, which range from quiet cafés and tiny bistros to beachside restaurants with panoramic views, highlight the Gulf Coast's vibrant culinary culture.

Camille's at Crystal Beach: Forget the tourist traps; Camille's is a local favorite for fresh seafood and inventive cuisine. Dive into their daily catch or enjoy melt-in-your-mouth sushi rolls. Arrive early; reservations are limited, and the wait will be worthwhile!

Red Onion: This hidden treasure offers a quiet, family-run setting ideal for a casual yet delicious supper. Red Onion promotes fresh, organic ingredients, resulting in delectable Mediterranean dishes that will keep you coming back for more.

Holi Indian Cuisine: Want a taste of India? Look no further than Holi. Take a culinary journey through India's diverse regions, where vegetarian and meat-based curries abound. The pleasant staff is happy to help you navigate the menu's spectacular assortment of tasty items.

Bric a Brac: This one could become your new favorite. While not exactly a secret, Bric a Brac is sometimes overlooked by visitors looking for a one-of-a-kind eating experience. Expect a pleasant ambiance and a meal that celebrates culinary inventiveness with fresh, seasonal ingredients.

Seaside Eateries: Savor the freshest seafood fished directly from the Gulf, with options ranging from basic shrimp and grits to creative ceviche and seafood towers.

Farm-to-Table Cuisine: Savor the Gulf Coast's farm-fresh flavors at restaurants that prioritize locally sourced ingredients and sustainable farming practices. From farm-fresh salads and artisanal cheese boards to grass-fed steaks and organic vegetables, these hidden gems showcase the region's fertile soil and stunning waterways.

Make reservations in advance, especially for dinner, since these hidden gems tend to fill up quickly with experienced locals. Consider dining outside of peak hours for a more quiet and peaceful experience, and don't be hesitant to ask your waitress for recommendations - they enjoy sharing their favorite meals with you!

Discover a world of charm and friendliness at Destin's best-kept secret restaurants, where charming decor and personalized service make dining as comfortable and inviting as it is delicious. From candlelight dinners and fireside discussions to outdoor dining under the stars, these hidden gems offer a romantic respite from the hustle and bustle of daily life.

Intimate bistros and cafés tucked away in hidden corners of Destin provide pleasant settings and appealing designs, setting the stage for an unforgettable dinner. Whether you're eating small dishes with friends or having a romantic meal for two, these hidden gems provide a culinary escape from the ordinary.

Use outside seating whenever possible to take advantage of the Gulf Coast's mild climate and breathtaking natural views. Don't forget to bring your camera to capture the breathtaking surroundings and unforgettable experiences that await you at these hidden culinary treasures.

Explore Destin's best-kept secret restaurants for a culinary adventure unlike any other, where each dish tells a story and every bite is a revelation. From imaginative fusion cuisine to classic comfort food with a twist, these hidden gems promise an unusual and delicious eating experience.

Chef's Specials: Take a chance and try the chef's specials, which are often influenced by seasonal ingredients, culinary trends, and the chef's creative whims. You never know what surprises await you, whether it's a daring flavor combination, an innovative presentation, or a dish that defies classification.

Local Favorites: Ask locals for recommendations and discover hidden culinary gems that may not be mentioned in tourist guides or review websites. Residents admire these hidden gems for their authenticity and charm, whether it's a hole-in-the-wall eatery known for its legendary breakfast sandwiches or a family-owned trattoria offering generations-old recipes.

When visiting Destin's best-kept secret restaurants, maintain an open mind and appreciate the spirit of gourmet adventure. Do not be afraid to try something new and unexpected; you never know when you'll discover your new favorite cuisine or restaurant!

Prepare to be stimulated and delighted by Destin's most popular gastronomic experiences: quiet coffee shops and authentic local cuisine. From artisan ales and exquisite pastries to powerful flavors and time-honored traditions passed down through generations, these culinary treasures offer a tantalizing glimpse into the Gulf Coast's rich culinary heritage.

Cozy coffee shops offer a warm welcome

Escape the hustle and bustle of daily life and enter the tranquil embrace of Destin's exquisite coffee shops, where the aroma of freshly brewed coffee and the sound of steaming espresso machines create a relaxing and introspective ambiance. Whether you're looking for a quiet place to work or study, catching up with friends over lattes and pastries, or simply enjoying some alone time with your favorite brew, these hidden gems promise a nice and friendly atmosphere that feels like home.

Artisanal Brews: Sip a cup of liquid gold made to perfection by committed baristas who take pride in their work. From silky lattes and creamy cappuccinos to powerful espressos and delectable pour-overs, Destin's coffee shops provide a diverse selection of specialized brews to suit every taste and preference.

Use the comfy surroundings and free Wi-Fi to catch up on work or study sessions, or simply relax and unwind with a good book or podcast. Consider trying a seasonal specialty drink or asking the barista for a recommendation; you might discover your new favorite brew!

Southern Comfort Food: Experience the warm embrace of Southern hospitality with hearty comfort food mainstays that both soothe the soul and satisfy the hunger. From crunchy fried chicken and fluffy biscuits to flavorful collard greens and creamy macaroni and cheese, these hidden gems offer a taste of home that will nourish and satisfy.

As you bid farewell to Destin's peaceful coffee shops and real local food, take with you not just memories of delicious brews and rich flavors, but also a greater appreciation for the culinary innovation and cultural diversity that pervade every corner of the Gulf Coast. Whether you spend the day sipping lattes in a quiet cafe or enjoying seafood delights in a hidden diner, these culinary treasures will always hold a special place in your heart.

4. RELAXATION & WELLNESS

4.1 Spa and Wellness Centres

Are you ready to go on a journey of regeneration and self-discovery? Prepare to be immersed in the tranquil oasis of Destin's top spas, yoga and meditation centers, and wellness retreats, where the stresses of everyday life drift away and inner peace and energy are restored.

From peaceful spa treatments and energizing yoga sessions to transformative wellness retreats, these sanctuaries provide a holistic approach to health and well-being that will leave you feeling refreshed, rejuvenated, and ready to live life to the fullest. Let's take a peek at the wellness choices in Destin.

The Spa at Silver Shells: This award-winning spa has a relaxing setting and focuses on individualized encounters. Relax with their famous massages or indulge in rejuvenating facials. They even provide couple's adventures, making it ideal for a romantic trip or a peaceful weekend with friends.

The Henderson Spa: Located within the magnificent Henderson Beach Resort, this spa is known for its cutting-edge facilities and professional therapists. Aromatherapy massages provide relaxation, while results-oriented facials refresh your skin. For a really holistic experience, look into their yoga and fitness sessions.

Surfside Spa: Looking for a beachside escape? Look no further than Surfside Spa. While enjoying a relaxing massage or an invigorating body scrub, listen to the quiet beat of the waves. They also provide a range of health treatments, such as hot stone therapy and hydrotherapy, to help you feel totally centered.

Avona's Massages offer a more personalized touch. This refuge specializes on therapeutic massage treatments that are adapted to your individual requirements. Whether you want pain treatment, stress reduction, or increased flexibility, their expert therapists can design a session that will leave you feeling your best.

Destin Pilates and Aerial: Looking to incorporate some movement into your fitness routine? Destin Pilates and Aerial provides a unique combination of pilates, yoga, and aerial fitness sessions. Strengthen your core, increase your flexibility, and have fun while doing it - all in a helpful and encouraging environment.

Find your center and reconnect with your inner self at Destin's yoga and meditation facilities, where ancient traditions and modern mindfulness merge in a perfect blend of movement, breath, and silence. Whether you're a seasoned yogi or a curious beginner, these centers offer a welcoming environment in which to discover the transformative power of yoga and meditation while fostering a sense of balance, strength, and inner peace.

Mindful Movement: Move gracefully through a series of yoga postures, syncing breath, and movement to relieve tension and stress while increasing strength, flexibility, and awareness. Whether you like the forceful flow of vinyasa or the peaceful embrace of yin yoga, these facilities provide classes for practitioners of all skill levels and capacities.

Peaceful Presence: Meditation and mindfulness can help you clear your mind and reconnect with your inner self. Guided meditation sessions help you develop present-moment awareness, reduce stress, and foster a sense of serenity and clarity throughout your life.

Experiment with different types of yoga and meditation practices to determine what works best for you. Consider attending seminars or special events held by the centers to improve your practice and meet like-minded people on the health journey.

A wellness retreat in the heart of Destin's natural beauty will take you on a journey of self-discovery and rejuvenation, complete with immersive activities and transformative practices to nourish your body, mind, and spirit. Whether you're searching for a weekend escape or a week-long immersion, these retreats provide a holistic approach to well-being that incorporates movement, nourishment, mindfulness, and connection in a supportive and loving environment.

Immerse yourself in a variety of holistic practices and healing approaches designed to improve your physical, mental, and spiritual health. From yoga and meditation to nutrition lessons and nature excursions, these retreats provide a comprehensive approach to wellness that addresses all elements of your being.

Community Connection: Make deep and meaningful connections with other retreat participants as you begin a journey of self-discovery and personal growth. Whether through group discussions, shared meals, or collaborative activities, these retreats foster a supportive community of like-minded individuals who inspire, uplift, and encourage one another on the path to wellness.

Avoid internet distractions and fully immerse yourself in the retreat experience. During your free time between scheduled events, explore Destin's natural beauty, journal, or simply rest and recharge in silent thought.

As you embark on your wellness journey in Destin, keep in mind that the path to optimal health and vitality is as individual as you.

Are you yearning for moments of peace amidst the hustle and bustle of everyday life? Look no further than Destin's tranquil places, which are hidden gems that offer a peaceful haven where you can unwind, recharge, and reconnect with nature and yourself. From serene beaches to calming parks and gardens, these calm havens invite you to slow down, breathe deeply, and absorb the beauty of the present moment. Let's have a quiet tour of Destin and discover the peaceful locations!

Quiet beaches for relaxation

Escape the crowds and visit Destin's serene beaches, where the soothing lull of the waves and soft caress of the sea breeze gives a peaceful haven for relaxation and meditation. Whether you're seeking silent contemplation or simply a moment of peace by the water's edge, these secluded stretches of beach are the perfect escape from the stresses of everyday life.

Solitary Shores: Discover quiet coves and solitary lengths of beach where you may relax in the sun while listening to the soothing sound of waves smashing on the coast. With fewer crowds and distractions, these tranquil beaches offer a serene setting for sunbathing, beachcombing, or simply watching the world go by.

Nature's Symphony: Immerse yourself in the natural symphony of the beach, where the tide's steady ebb and flow provides a soothing backdrop. Close your eyes and allow the sounds of seagulls calling overhead, waves breaking on the beach, and soft winds rustling through the palm trees to transport you to a state of profound relaxation and inner tranquility.

Arrive early in the morning or late in the afternoon to avoid crowds and enjoy the beach at its most serene. Bring a beach chair, an umbrella, and your favorite book or music to help you unwind, and remember to stay hydrated and sun-safe.

Serene parks and gardens showcase nature's splendor

Escape the city and reconnect with nature in Destin's serene parks and gardens, where lush foliage, beautiful blooms, and tranquil water features create a stunning backdrop for relaxation and restoration. Whether you're walking down winding trails, picnicking in protected woodlands, or simply sitting quietly and absorbing the beauty around you, these hidden gems offer a welcome respite from the hustle and bustle of everyday life.

Botanical Bliss: Travel through colorful botanical gardens and nature preserves to see the beauty and diversity of native flora and fauna. These tranquil surroundings, which range from vivid wildflowers and towering trees to flowing streams and quiet ponds, are both a feast for the senses and a haven for tired spirits seeking solace in nature.

Beautiful Strolls: Put on your walking shoes and take a stroll along meandering walkways and trails that wind through lush vegetation and lovely scenery. Whether you're searching for a brisk morning walk to wake up your senses or a leisurely evening stroll to unwind after a long day, these calm parks and gardens are the perfect place for outdoor exploration and relaxation.

Bring a picnic basket with your favorite food and beverages for a quiet supper surrounded by nature's beauty. Consider bringing a camera or a journal to document the beauty of your surroundings and inspire your creativity.

Peaceful Picnic Areas: Bringing Food and Nature Together

Enjoy the simple pleasures of life with a leisurely picnic in one of Destin's serene outdoor areas, where lush green grass, leafy trees, and breathtaking views provide the ideal atmosphere for al fresco dining and relaxation. Whether you're having a romantic meal for two, gathering with friends and family for a holiday feast, or simply enjoying a quiet moment of solitude, these peaceful picnic sites offer a welcome break from the hustle and bustle of everyday life.

Spread out a blanket and get ready for a magnificent picnic in one of Destin's stunning outdoor settings, which range from coastal parks and seaside groves to shady meadows and gorgeous views. With plenty of space to spread out and stunning views to enjoy, these quiet picnic areas offer a tranquil setting for outdoor meals and recreation.

Gourmet Delights: Fill a picnic basket with gourmet delicacies such as artisanal cheeses, fresh fruit, crusty bread, savory sandwiches, and decadent desserts. Whether you opt for handmade treats or gourmet sweets from a local deli, these scrumptious nibbles are sure to enhance your outdoor dining experience and satisfy your taste buds.

Arrive early to get a decent picnic spot avoid the crowds, and pack enough sunscreen, insect spray, and other supplies for a calm and enjoyable experience. Consider bringing some outside games or diversions for after lunch, such as frisbee, bocce ball, or a deck of cards.

4.2 Mindfulness Activities

Are you willing to immerse yourself in the present moment and open your eyes to the wonders of the world around you? Welcome to Destin, where mindfulness techniques promote relaxation, pleasure, and a strong connection with nature and oneself. From serene sunset viewing spots to guided nature hikes and inspiring art and craft classes, these activities encourage you to slow down, breathe deeply, and appreciate every moment with wonder and gratitude. Let's go on a mindfulness journey and discover the transformative power of being completely present in the moment.

Sunset Viewing Locations: Experience the spectacular splendor of Destin's famed sunsets from the best vantage point, as the sky explodes with gold, crimson, and indigo hues, and the soft murmur of the waves provides a peaceful soundtrack for relaxation and introspection.

Scenic Overlooks: Look for elevated vantage points, such as coastal cliffs or waterfront promenades, that provide panoramic views of the horizon, allowing you to witness the entire spectacle of the sun setting into the glittering waters of the Gulf.

Tranquil Beaches: Relax on the smooth sands of a secluded beach or quiet cove and watch as the sky transforms into a canvas of vibrant colors, painting the horizon in pink, orange, and purple as it reflects off the calm waters beneath.

Arrive early to secure a prime viewing spot and allow plenty of time to appreciate the beauty of the sunset. To make the most of your viewing experience, bring a picnic blanket, refreshments, and beverages, as well as a camera to capture the spectacular moments.

Guided Nature Walks: Discover the Heart of the Wilderness

Take a guided nature walk to immerse yourself in the pure splendor of Destin's natural settings, where towering trees, twisting pathways, and abundant wildlife weave a tapestry of sights, sounds, and feelings that awaken and nourish the spirit.

Expert Guidance: Join professional guides and naturalists on an immersive tour of the region's various ecosystems, where they will provide fascinating insights into the flora, fauna, and geological formations that distinguish each environment.

Mindful Exploration: Take your time and enjoy each step as you walk down meandering paths, taking in the exquisite patterns of sunlight streaming through the canopy, the delicate blossoms of wildflowers, and the graceful motions of birds and butterflies fluttering among the trees.

Dress comfortably and wear sturdy shoes designed for walking on rough terrain. Bring a water bottle, sunscreen, bug repellent, and a hat to keep comfortable and safe on your outdoor journey. Don't forget to bring a camera or binoculars for close-up shots of animals and breathtaking panoramas along the route.

Art and Craft Workshops: Join hands-on art and craft programs that will inspire, motivate, and empower you to express yourself through color, texture, and shape. Whether you're painting air, sculpting with clay, or making handcrafted jewelry, these immersive events provide a therapeutic avenue for self-expression as well as a joyful celebration of creativity.

Creative Expression: Release your inhibitions and succumb to the flow of inspiration as you explore various materials and methods under the supervision of professional artists and professors who will foster your abilities and encourage your artistic vision to grow.

Connect with other creatives and like-minded individuals as you partake in the excitement of artistic exploration and discovery, exchanging ideas, inspiration, and encouragement in a friendly and uplifting setting.

Embrace the spirit of exploration and give yourself permission to play and explore without judgment or expectation. Don't stress about producing a masterpiece; instead, concentrate on the process of creation and the delight of self-expression. Consider putting your completed artwork in your house as a reminder of your creative journey and the beauty of the moment.

5: FAMILY FUN

5.1 Kids-Friendly Beaches in Destin

Ready to create wonderful experiences with your children under the sun? Destin's kid-friendly beaches provide an abundance of excitement, adventure, and unlimited entertainment for the entire family. From shallow water havens ideal for small toes to beaches with playgrounds and picnic areas, these sandy coastlines offer a day of laughing, exploration, and delight that your children will remember for years. Let's pack the sunscreen, snacks, and beach toys and embark on a journey of surprise and joy!

Shallow Water Beaches: Splash and Play Safety

Looking for beaches where your children may safely splash and play in the shallows? Destin provides various alternatives for mild waves and shallow seas, allowing even the smallest beachgoers to dip their toes and create sandcastles to their hearts' content.

Henderson Beach State Park: With its pure white sands and tranquil, clear seas, Henderson Beach State Park is ideal for families with small children. The shallow entry into the ocean allows children to safely wade and splash, while parents may rest and enjoy the sun on the soft dunes nearby.

Crystal Beach is another popular family destination, noted for its tranquil seas and low surf. The gentle descent into the water is great for young swimmers and beginning paddlers, and the smooth sands provide ample room for sandcastle building and beach activities.

Bring inflatable floaties or water wings for extra safety and peace of mind, and keep an eye on your children at all times, especially near the water's edge. Pack beach equipment such as buckets, shovels, and sand molds to have hours of sandy fun!

Beaches with Playgrounds: Sand Castles and Slides by the Sea

Combine beach time with playground fun at Destin's beaches, which have on-site playgrounds where kids can climb, slide, and swing to their hearts' delight in between dips in the water and sandcastle building.

Norriego Point, located at the entrance to Destin Harbor, is not only a popular beach location, but it also has a playground where children can burn off excess energy before or after their beach excursions. With swings, slides, and climbing structures overlooking the bay, it's a great place for kids of all ages to play and explore.

James Lee Park: Nestled along the stunning coastline of the Gulf of Mexico, James Lee Park offers not only beautiful beaches but also a covered playground area where children may take a break from the sand and waves to enjoy some playground activities. Allow your children kids climb, slide, and swing to their hearts' delight as you rest nearby and admire the breathtaking coastal views.

Bring a beach umbrella or pop-up tent to give shade to children as they play, and don't forget to bring plenty of drinks and snacks to keep everyone hydrated and ready for fun. Consider going to the playground at off-peak hours to minimize crowds and optimize fun.

Picnic-Friendly Locations: Lunchtime Adventures by the Sea

Turn your beach day into a picnic experience by visiting Destin's picnic-friendly sites, which have covered pavilions, grassy lawns, and sandy shorelines that are ideal for a family feast.

Crystal Sands Beach: Spread out a blanket or set up camp at one of the picnic tables tucked amid the dunes to enjoy a leisurely meal while basking in the sun and sea wind. After your dinner, walk down the beach and look for seashells with your children.

James Lee Park: With its covered picnic pavilions and picturesque coastline vistas, James Lee Park is an excellent location for a family lunch by the sea. Pack a cooler with sandwiches, snacks, and cold drinks, and enjoy a relaxed day of seaside eating and quality time with your loved ones.

Bring a cooler full of kid-friendly food and drinks, as well as sunscreen, hats, and sunglasses, to keep everyone safe from the sun. Consider bringing a beach umbrella or pop-up tent for additional shade, and remember to properly clean up and dispose of rubbish to help keep our beaches clean and beautiful.

5.2 Family attractions

Discover Destin's Top Attractions for Families

Prepare for an exciting family vacation in Destin, where thrilling rides, interesting marine life, and nonstop entertainment await at some of the city's most popular attractions. Whether you're splashing around at Big Kahuna's Water and Adventure Park, marveling at marine wonders at Gulfarium Marine Adventure Park, or racing around The Track Family Fun Park, these family-friendly destinations promise a day of laughter, excitement, and treasured memories to last a lifetime. Let's take a whirlwind tour of family activities and discover the enchantment that awaits you in Destin!

- **Big Kahuna's Water and Adventure Park**

Prepare to fight the heat and make a splash at Big Kahuna's Water and Adventure Park, where thrills and excitement are around every turn. From twisting water slides and sluggish rivers to wave pools and children's play zones, this tropical paradise has something for everyone.

Thrilling Water Rides: Feel the rush of excitement as you plunge towering water slides, twist and turn through twisting flumes, and battle the waves in the wave pool. With attractions such as the Kowabunga Racer, Jumanji, and the Honolulu Half Pipe, thrill-seekers of all ages will find plenty of heart-pounding adrenaline.

Family-Friendly Attractions: Children will enjoy splashing and playing in the kiddie pools and interactive water play zones, while parents can chill in the lazy river or soak up some rays on the sun-drenched balcony. Big Kahuna offers lots of covered lounging places, dining options, and facilities to provide a pleasant and pleasurable visit for the entire family.

Arrive early to beat the crowds, and consider purchasing tickets online ahead of time to avoid long queues. Don't forget to bring sunscreen, towels, and lots of water to remain hydrated throughout the day, and look for special events and promotions to add value and excitement.

Gulfarium - Marine Adventure Park

At Gulfarium Marine Adventure Park, visitors may take an exciting voyage into the underwater realm, where intriguing marine species and interactive displays provide an up-close and personal look at the ocean's treasures. This marine park offers a day of exploration and enjoyment for the entire family, with playful dolphins and majestic sea lions, as well as beautiful fish and unusual birds.

Dolphin & Sea Lion displays: Be charmed by the elegance and intellect of dolphins and sea lions as they perform dazzling acrobatics, amusing antics, and mind-blowing stunts throughout daily displays and presentations. Get a front-row seat to the action and see the beauty and agility of these amazing marine creatures.

Interactive Exhibits: Immerse yourself in the realm of marine life by touching, feeding, and learning about stingrays, turtles, and sharks. Get up close and personal with these amazing species, and you'll understand why ocean conservation is so important.

Arrive early to get parking make the most of your visit, and check the park's schedule for showtimes and feeding times to maximize your experience. Consider purchasing a picture package to record unique moments with the animals, and don't forget to stop by the gift store for mementos to remember the day by.

The Track Family Fun Park: Race to Adventure

Buckle up and prepare for high-speed thrills and excitement at The Track Family Fun Park, where go-kart tracks, bumper boats, and mini-golf courses offer hours of adrenaline-fueled entertainment for the entire family. This action-packed park has activities for all ages and interests, ensuring a day of fun, competition, and wonderful memories.

Strap in and crank your engines as you race over hairpin twists, banked curves, and straightaways on a variety of go-kart circuits suitable for drivers of all ages and ability levels. Whether you're a speed maniac seeking a challenge or a new driver just getting started, The Track has tracks to fit your style and preferences.

Family-Friendly Attractions: In addition to go-karts, The Track has several additional attractions and activities to keep the entire family engaged, including bumper boats, mini-golf courses, batting cages, and arcade games. With indoor and outdoor activities available year-round, there's never a dull moment at this popular family attraction.

For the best value and most enjoyment, consider getting a multi-attraction pass or an unlimited ride wristband. Beat the heat by going in the morning or evening when temps are lower, and remember to take pauses to remain hydrated and reapply sunscreen throughout the day. Remember to record memories with photographs and videos so you can remember the excitement long after your stay.

5.3 Educational Experiences

Prepare to embark on an adventure of exploration and discovery as you enter the interesting world of educational experiences in Destin. From thrilling sea life safaris to hands-on scientific displays and interactive learning centers, these places provide visitors of all ages with numerous chances to learn, explore, and be inspired by the marvels of nature and beyond. So bring your curiosity and sense of wonder, and prepare for a journey that will pique your interest and leave you with a renewed respect for the world around you!

Sea Life Safaris: Explore the Marine Kingdom

Set sail on a sea life safari for an amazing journey of discovery across the pristine waters of the Gulf of Mexico. These informative excursions, conducted by trained guides and marine specialists, provide a unique opportunity to see a variety of marine creatures up close while learning about their habitats, behaviors, and conservation efforts.

Marine experiences: From playful dolphins and magnificent sea turtles to beautiful manatees and elusive sharks, each marine life safari offers exciting experiences with some of the ocean's most renowned creatures. Listen as experienced guides give intriguing insights and tales about the species you see, helping you appreciate their value to marine ecosystems and our world as a whole.

Hands-On Learning: Participate in instructional activities and interactive experiences that make marine science more interesting and relevant. Whether you're taking part in a dolphin research study, completing water quality checks, or snorkeling with marine scientists, these immersive activities provide a unique opportunity to learn and contribute to current conservation efforts.

Bring a waterproof camera or smartphone to record images and videos of your marine encounters, and remember to take sunscreen, sunglasses, and a hat to protect yourself from the sun. Consider arranging a private charter or tailoring your safari trip to your interests and tastes for an even more customized educational encounter!

Emerald Coast Science Center: Ignite Your Curiosity

Prepare to pique your interest and release your inner scientist at the Emerald Coast Science Center, where hands-on exhibits, interactive demonstrations, and educational events await interested minds of all ages. This vibrant scientific center, which focuses on STEM (science, technology, engineering, and mathematics) education, provides a portal to exploration and a world of learning that is both thrilling and instructive.

Interactive displays: Enter a world of wonder and investigation as you walk through a variety of interactive displays covering a wide range of scientific disciplines, from physics and chemistry to biology and astronomy. Experiment with electricity, investigate natural forces and marvel at the marvels of the world while participating in hands-on activities and demonstrations that make learning enjoyable and engaging.

Educational Programs: Learn more about STEM ideas through educational programs and seminars offered by experienced educators and scientific lovers. The Emerald Coast Scientific Center has something for everyone to enjoy and learn from, including robotics and coding programs, scientific camps, and family-friendly activities.

Plan your visit around special events and themed exhibitions for a more immersive and engaging experience, and check the science center's website for hours of operation, ticket pricing, and forthcoming programming. Consider becoming a member to receive unique perks and savings on future trips, and don't forget to pick up some science-themed souvenirs from the gift store to help you learn at home!

Children's Museums and Learning Centers: Play, Learn, and Grow

A visit to one of Destin's children's museums and learning centers will fuel your child's imagination and inspire their curiosity, with interactive exhibits, innovative play spaces, and educational programs offering unlimited chances for exploration, discovery, and development. From hands-on scientific experiments and art activities to role-playing adventures and sensory play, these venues provide a plethora of opportunities to excite young minds and nurture a lifetime love of education.

Discovery Zones: Allow your children to express their creativity and curiosity in discovery zones filled with interactive exhibits and play spaces that promote inquiry and experimentation. From building blocks and sensory tables to pretend play spaces and painting studios, there are plenty of activities to keep young minds and bodies engaged in a fun and instructive way.

Participate in educator-led programs and workshops that provide guided learning experiences and hands-on activities to help youngsters comprehend science, art, history, and other topics. Whether it's a STEM workshop, an art class, or a history-themed treasure hunt, these programs allow youngsters to acquire new skills, meet new people, and build memorable experiences.

Encourage your child to ask questions, explore freely, and pursue their interests while they explore the museum's exhibits and activities. Take advantage of family memberships or cheap admission days to make repeat visits more economical, and consider hosting your child's next birthday party or special event at the museum for a fun and unforgettable occasion!

So seize the chance to explore, discover, and grow as a family, and use the wonders of science, nature, and imagination to lead you on a lifelong journey of learning and discovery. Destin offers an abundance of educational opportunities, including sea life safaris, scientific centers, and children's museums. So, what are you waiting for? Let the learning begin!

6: DINING AND NIGHTLIFE

6.1 The Top Restaurants in Destin

Destin, where the food scene is as active and diverse as the stunning beaches that surround this tropical haven. Destin's finest restaurants range from fresh seafood delicacies to sophisticated fine dining and laid-back casual cafes, providing a feast for the senses and an amazing dining experience. Prepare to go on a delicious journey that will fulfill your appetites, delight your taste buds, and keep you coming back for more!

Seafood Specialties: Tasting the Ocean's Bounty

In Destin, the seafood is as fresh as the ocean wind, and the gourmet masterpieces made with the day's catch are nothing short of outstanding. Whether you want luscious shrimp, soft crab, or flaky fish, these seafood restaurants create meals that highlight Gulf tastes with passion and accuracy.

Dewey Destin's Seafood Restaurant: Located on the water's edge, Dewey Destin's provides a relaxed, down-home ambiance where the seafood is the star of the show. Feast on their famed fried shrimp, wonderfully seasoned crab legs, or a traditional grouper sandwich while admiring the harbor vistas. Don't miss the hush puppies; they're renowned.

Boshamps Seafood & Oyster House: With its colorful waterfront backdrop and cuisine packed with Gulf-to-table pleasures, Boshamps is a seafood lover's dream. Indulge in the Oysters Bienville, taste the richness of the smoked tuna dip, or dig into a hefty meal of shrimp and grits. Pair your meal with a refreshing beverage from their vast drink menu and enjoy the vibrant ambiance.

The Back Porch, a Destin institution since 1974, is known for its delicious, locally sourced seafood and laid-back atmosphere. Enjoy a hearty helping of Amberjack steak, grilled or blackened to perfection, or appreciate the delicate aromas of their renowned chargrilled Gulf shrimp. With a view of the beach and the sound of the waves, this dining experience embodies the spirit of Destin.

Arrive early to secure a good riverfront spot, particularly during busy eating hours. Don't be afraid to ask your server for the day's freshest fish or house specialties; they'll guide you to the best options. And, of course, bring an appetite.

Fine Dining Options

For those looking for a more refined dining experience, Destin's fine dining restaurants combine sophisticated decor, superb service, and culinary talent to elevate every meal to a memorable occasion. These restaurants are ideal for a romantic evening, a special occasion, or simply treating yourself to the finer things.

Marina Cafe, which overlooks the gorgeous Destin Harbor, offers spectacular vistas as well as a contemporary menu that reflects the finest of both land and sea. Enjoy meals such as pan-seared scallops, delicious lobster ravioli, and masterfully made filet mignon. Marina Cafe offers a large wine selection and superb service, ensuring an evening of elegance and enjoyment.

Beach Walk Cafe, located in the Henderson Park Inn, provides a relaxing, seaside dining experience that is both intimate and exquisite. Enjoy the tastes of the Gulf with dishes like pecan-crusted grouper, the chef's daily fresh catch, or the decadent crab-crusted blackened mahi. For an added touch of romanticism, choose the "Toes in the Sand" dining experience, which allows you to eat directly on the beach.

Seagar's Prime Steaks & Seafood: For those who enjoy the best steaks and seafood, Seagar's provides an unrivaled dining experience. Seagar's, known for its USDA Prime steaks, fresh seafood, and enormous wine cellar, always delivers quality to every meal. Try the traditional surf and turf, the buttery lobster tail, or the house-aged ribeye. Seagar's is Destin's finest dining establishment, with a sophisticated, beautiful setting and superb service.

Reservations are generally suggested for these upscale dining establishments, especially on weekends and during peak season. Dress to impress and take your time with each meal; great dining is all about the experience. Do not hesitate to ask the sommelier for wine pairings that will properly suit your meal.

Casual Eateries: Relax and Enjoy

When you're looking for a relaxing, laid-back eating experience without sacrificing taste or quality, Destin's casual cafes provide a pleasant ambiance and excellent meals that will make you feel right at home. These restaurants are ideal for family trips, fast eats, or a great night out with friends. They deliver big on food and warmth.

Harry T's Lighthouse: Located in HarborWalk Village, Harry T's provides a delightful, nautical-themed eating experience with a menu full of fan favorites. From delectable fish tacos and juicy burgers to fresh seafood platters, there's something for everybody. Harry T's is an excellent choice for casual eating with a twist, thanks to its lively environment, magnificent harbor views, and live music.

The Donut Hole: More than simply a breakfast establishment, The Donut Hole is a cherished Destin staple that serves substantial comfort cuisine all day. Begin your day with their famed donuts and pastries, or dig into a dish of fluffy pancakes, a loaded omelet, or a southern-style breakfast buffet. For lunch and supper, they provide staples such as chicken fried steak, turkey with dressing, and a variety of sandwiches and salads.

Fudpucker's Beachside Bar & Grill: A must-see for families, Fudpucker's has a fun environment and a cuisine that will suit the entire crew. Kids will enjoy the live alligator display and the opportunity to feed these fascinating creatures. Meanwhile, savor delicious delicacies such as the Fudburger, seafood platters, and tropical beverages. Fudpucker's is all about having fun, eating delicious food, and spending time with family.

Casual eateries in Destin are sometimes first-come, first-served, so plan if you're going during busy hours. Bring the kids and enjoy the casual atmosphere; many of these establishments are family-friendly and have excellent kids' menus. Check for live music and unique activities to enhance your dining experience.

Regardless of your eating choices, Destin's greatest restaurants guarantee a culinary experience full of flavor, excitement, and unforgettable moments. Whether you're relishing the freshest seafood, experiencing a sophisticated fine dining experience, or unwinding at a casual diner, each meal takes you closer to the heart and soul of Destin's thriving culinary scene. So, assemble your loved ones, bring your hunger, and prepare to go on a culinary journey you'll remember long after the final taste.

Savor the local flavors of Destin. A culinary adventure awaits.

Immerse yourself in Destin's wonderful and unique flavors, where fresh, locally sourced products and culinary ingenuity combine to create exceptional dining experiences. Destin is a feast for the senses, celebrating the finest of coastal living with famous must-try cuisine, busy farmers markets, colorful culinary festivals, and the distinct appeal of beachside eating. Prepare to go on a delicious adventure that will take you to the heart and soul of Destin's culinary scene.

6.2 Must-Try Local Cuisine

Destin's cuisine is a real expression of its seaside past, combining fresh seafood with Southern comfort and creative twists. Here are some must-try meals that embody Destin's culinary identity:

The grouper sandwich, a Destin favorite, reflects the town's strong fishing past. This sandwich, which is usually grilled, blackened, or fried, consists of flaky, supple grouper fillet snuggled on soft bread and is frequently served with tartar sauce, lettuce, and tomato. It's a simple yet tasty recipe that highlights the freshness of the Gulf's riches.

> Shrimp and Grits: A Southern classic with a coastal twist, shrimp and grits in Destin are a must-try for any seafood enthusiast. Juicy, plump shrimp are sautéed in a flavorful sauce and served over creamy, cheesy grits. This comfortable dish is frequently served with crispy bacon, green onions, and a dash of spicy sauce, resulting in a wonderful combination of flavors and textures.

Oysters Rockefeller: For a taste of luxury, try Oysters Rockefeller, which mixes the saline sweetness of fresh oysters with a rich, savory topping of spinach, cheese, and breadcrumbs that is cooked to perfection. This meal, whether served as an appetizer or main course, exemplifies Destin's culinary innovation and love of fish.

Don't miss out on trying these delicacies at Dewey Destin's Seafood Restaurant, The Back Porch, or Boshamps Seafood & Oyster House, which are all local favorites. To ensure a genuine and memorable dining experience, ask your waitress for recommendations on the day's freshest fish.

Farmers' markets and food festivals: fresh and flavorful

Destin's farmers markets and food festivals provide a colorful display of the region's freshest produce, artisanal items, and culinary abilities. These events are a must-see for foodies looking to enjoy local delicacies and engage with the community.

Destin Farmers Market: Held weekly, the Destin Farmers Market is a thriving center of activity where local farmers, artists, and food sellers join together to showcase their best products. Browse vendors selling fresh fruits and vegetables, handmade jams & jellies, baked products, and more. It's the ideal spot to pick up picnic supplies or a keepsake to take home.

The annual Seafood Festival, which celebrates Destin's historical fishing legacy, is a gastronomic highlight. This vibrant event includes culinary demos, live music, and, of course, a wide variety of seafood delicacies to try. From shrimp and oysters to crab and fish, it's a seafood lover's dream that also benefits local fishermen and the community.

HarborWalk Village Events: Throughout the year, HarborWalk Village holds several food-related events, such as wine and food festivals, where visitors may sample gourmet snacks, local wines, and craft brews while admiring the gorgeous views of Destin Harbor. These events provide an excellent opportunity to sample the local food scene in a festive and enjoyable setting.

Arrive early at farmers' markets and festivals to avoid crowds and obtain the freshest produce. Bring cash for quick transactions, and don't forget to try as many different cuisines as you can; it's the greatest way to discover Destin's unique flavors.

Beachfront Dining: Feast with a View

Nothing beats eating with the sound of waves crashing and the smell of seawater in the air. Beachfront dining in Destin provides not only wonderful meals but also a memorable atmosphere that adds to the enjoyment of each mouthful.

The Crab Trap: Located close to the beach, The Crab Trap provides breathtaking views of the Gulf as well as a cuisine full of seafood classics. Enjoy crab legs, shrimp boils, and fish tacos while watching the sunset over the horizon. The easygoing, beachy atmosphere makes it ideal for family gatherings or romantic dinners.

Pompano Joe's: This vibrant beachside restaurant is a Destin institution, noted for its Caribbean-inspired fish cuisine and upbeat ambiance. Enjoy coconut shrimp, mahi-mahi sandwiches, and seafood platters while seeing the green seas from a panoramic vista. The relaxed atmosphere and pleasant service make it a must-see for anybody wishing to enjoy a dinner by the sea.

Harbor Docks offers a more upmarket seaside eating experience, combining fresh, locally produced seafood with breathtaking harbor views. Enjoy sushi rolls, grilled seafood, and chef specialties in a refined yet inviting setting. The outside deck is ideal for an alfresco supper and provides a front-row view of Destin's stunning shoreline.

Make reservations wherever feasible, especially for supper, to get the finest seats with a view. Dress comfortably and pack a small jacket for chilly evenings. And don't rush; take your time and enjoy the sights, tastes, and companionship.

Destin's unique tastes provide a gastronomic excursion that highlights the Gulf's abundant abundance, the chefs' ingenuity, and the vibrant community spirit. Whether you're indulging in must-try delicacies, visiting farmers markets and food festivals, or enjoying a dinner with a beachfront view, every mouthful demonstrates the love and passion that make Destin's culinary scene so unique. So come hungry and prepared to experience the amazing and different sensations that greet you in this seaside paradise!

6.3 Destiny After Dark

When the sun sets over Destin's emerald waters, a new world of excitement and entertainment emerges. Destin's nightlife offers something for everyone, whether you want to dance the night away in a vibrant bar, listen to live music beneath the stars, or take a quiet sunset cruise. Prepare to enjoy Destin's bustling, diversified, and fascinating after-dark scene, which contributes to the city's enchanting atmosphere.

Bars and clubs: dance, drink, and delight

Destin's pubs and clubs provide a diverse range of atmospheres, from casual beach bars to high-energy dance clubs. There's a location for you, whether you want to sip a handmade cocktail, drink a refreshing beer with pals, or dance the night away.

AJ's Seafood & Oyster Bar: A Destin nightlife mainstay, AJ's is recognized for its boisterous environment, delicious cuisine, and breathtaking views of the bay. By day, it's a popular destination for fresh seafood; at night, it morphs into a crowded bar with live music, dancing, and themed events. Grab a drink, join the party, and let the good times roll.

The Red Door Saloon is the place to go if you want a more relaxed atmosphere. This oceanfront pub has a relaxing, friendly ambiance, a great range of beers, inventive drinks, and an interesting design that welcomes you to unwind. Challenge your pals to a game of pool or darts, and enjoy the relaxed, inviting atmosphere.

Bric à Brac: If you enjoy dancing, visit Bric à Brac, a dynamic restaurant and nightclub with a mix of live bands and DJ performances. Bric à Brac's colorful atmosphere, superb food, and active dance floor ensure a memorable night out. Dance to your heart's delight and meet new people while you take up the lively vibe.

Pro Tip: Look at each venue's schedule for live music and special events. Arrive early to secure a nice space, especially on weekends, and always bring a designated driver or utilize a ridesharing service to guarantee a safe night out.

Live Music Venues: Tunes Under The Stars

Destin's live music scene is as eclectic as it is energetic, with rock, country, jazz, and reggae. Here are some of the best places to see live music and have a good time.

HarborWalk Village: This waterfront destination is not only fantastic for shopping and dining, but it is also a popular site for live music. HarborWalk Village presents outdoor concerts year-round, including both local and national performers. Enjoy the music while you wander around the port, get a drink at one of the neighboring pubs, and soak up the lively scene.

Club LA, known for its amazing mix of live bands and musicians, is a must-see for music fans. From rock and metal to country and blues, this venue provides an intimate atmosphere in which to get up close and personal with the performances. Check their schedule for future performances and get ready for an incredible night of music.

The Village Door Music Hall, located in the Village of Baytowne Wharf, is known for its live music, dancing, and active nightlife. Enjoy performances by amazing musicians while drinking beverages and dancing the night away. The venue's explosive ambiance and high-quality sound system make it a popular choice for live entertainment in Destin.

Follow your favorite venues on social media to keep informed about future concerts and ticket sales. To minimize disappointment, consider getting tickets in advance for popular acts. Don't forget to wear comfy shoes; you'll want to dance all night!

Sunset cruises and evening entertainment: For a more relaxing but equally enchanting evening, Destin has several sunset cruises and evening entertainment options that allow you to take in the splendor of the coast while enjoying fantastic company and entertainment.

SunVenture Cruises: Take a sunset cruise with SunVenture Cruises and enjoy the spectacular beauty of the Gulf as the sun sets below the horizon. Enjoy a relaxed evening on the ocean with breathtaking views, cool beverages, and the opportunity to see dolphins. It's the ideal way to relax and enjoy Destin's natural beauty.

Southern Star Dolphin Cruises: On a Southern Star cruise, you may observe dolphins while enjoying a lovely sunset. These family-friendly tours allow you to witness lively dolphins in their natural environment while admiring the tranquil sunset vistas. With skilled experts and a comfortable boat, the experience is both instructive and pleasant.

HarborWalk Village Fireworks: Throughout the summer, HarborWalk Village illuminates the night sky with breathtaking fireworks displays. Take a seat at one of the riverside restaurants or locate a comfortable area along the port to enjoy the display. It's a lovely way to conclude the evening, with vivid bursts of color flashing off the ocean.

Book your sunset cruise in advance, especially during high seasons, to ensure a place. Bring a light jacket or sweater because it can get windy on the ocean after dark. Don't forget your camera; the sights are certainly Instagram-worthy.

Whatever way you choose to spend your nights in Destin, the exciting nightlife, compelling live music, and calm sunset cruises guarantee to make great memories. Accept the intensity, take in the beauty, and savor every minute as Destin's nightlife unfolds before you. Whether you're dancing beneath the stars, swaying to live music, or drifting down the coast on a sunset cruise, you're in for a memorable evening. Cheers to memorable nights in Destin!

7: SHOPPING

7.1 Destin's Premier Shopping Districts

Destin isn't only about beautiful beaches and exciting water activities; it's also a shopping heaven! Whether you're looking for high-end clothes, unique local treasures, or great deals, Destin's retail areas provide something for everyone. Prepare to discover bustling shopping destinations that blend retail therapy with a delicious dose of fun, food, and entertainment.

Destin Commons: A Shoppers Delight

Destin Commons is more than a retail mall; it's an experience. This open-air lifestyle center has a variety of popular retail establishments, local boutiques, and delectable dining options, all situated in a beautifully designed environment that beckons you to stay and explore.

Shop: Destin Commons is home to a diverse range of retailers, including national favorites such as Sephora, H&M, and Bass Pro Shop. Whether you're looking to update your clothing, buy beauty items, or prepare for an outdoor excursion, you'll find everything you need. Don't pass up unusual businesses like Earthbound Trading Company for offbeat items and Southern Living Store for attractive home décor and gifts.

Dine: After a successful shopping adventure, reward yourself with a nice dinner at one of Destin Commons' numerous restaurants. Take a fast nibble at Chipotle or Which Wich, a casual dinner at Redbrick Pizza or Zoe's Kitchen, or a formal dining experience at Uncle Buck's Fishbowl & Grill, which combines seafood and bowling under one roof.

Destin Commons is more than simply a shopping and eating destination; it is also a place to have fun and be entertained. Catch the newest movie at the AMC cinema, let the kids play on the splash pad and playground, or simply walk around the beautifully planted courtyards. The bustling environment, along with seasonal events and live performances, guarantees that there is always something fascinating going on at Destin Commons.

Visit the customer service desk to obtain a directory and information on current deals. Keep an eye out for seasonal specials and events to find the finest shopping deals and family activities.

Silver Sands Premium Outlets: Deals galore

For those who enjoy a good deal, Silver Sands Premium Outlets is a must-see. As one of the country's major outlet malls, it has an excellent assortment of retailers that sell top brands at reduced costs.

Shop: Silver Sands has over 100 designer and name-brand outlet stores, making it an ideal destination for discerning shoppers. Find great prices on high-end apparel like Michael Kors, Coach, and Kate Spade. Upgrade your sporting apparel with Nike, Under Armour, and Adidas, or get wonderful home products at Le Creuset and Kitchen

Collection. With so many selections, you're bound to discover fantastic prices on anything from apparel and accessories to housewares and gifts.

Dine: Shopping works up an appetite, and Silver Sands provides a variety of food alternatives to satisfy. Grab a quick lunch at Auntie Anne's or Starbucks before sitting down for dinner at Carrabba's Italian Grill or Panera Bread. For a sweet treat, visit Godiva Chocolatier or Mrs. Fields for delectable cookies and confections.

Relax: Take a break from shopping to unwind in one of the shaded resting areas or beautifully planted courtyards. Silver Sands also provides handy services like stroller rentals, free Wi-Fi, and a playground for children, guaranteeing a pleasant and fun shopping experience for the entire family.

Join the VIP Shopper Club on the Silver Sands website to obtain unique discounts and deals. Visit throughout the week for a more peaceful shopping experience, since weekends may be very hectic.

HarborWalk Village mixes the ambiance of a coastal promenade with a distinctive retail experience. Located along the picturesque Destin Harbor, this dynamic location provides a variety of shopping, dining, and entertainment options, all with breathtaking views of the sea.

Shop: HarborWalk Village has several specialty stores and boutiques where you may purchase unusual gifts, beachwear, and local art. Explore establishments such as Kitty Hawk Kites for kites and outdoor goods, Aloha Surf Company for fashionable beachwear, and Naples Soap Company for natural bath and body items. Each business has its unique offering, making shopping here an enjoyable treasure hunt.

Dine: Savor the tastes of the Gulf Coast at one of the numerous restaurants in HarborWalk Village. Enjoy fresh fish at Harry T's Lighthouse or Jackacuda's Fish & Sushi, delicious burgers at Margaritaville, and a luscious ice cream cone from The Fudgery. There are several waterfront eating options available, so you can have a nice dinner while taking in the amazing harbor views.

Play: HarborWalk Village is more than simply a shopping and eating destination; it's also a hub for entertainment and activity. Take a stroll down the boardwalk, watch the boats come and go, or participate in activities like zip-lining, rock climbing, and dolphin excursions. The town also organizes several events throughout the year, such as live music, fireworks, and festivals, making it an exciting place to visit day or night.

Plan your visit around the weekly fireworks displays in the summer for an added dose of entertainment. Arrive early to locate parking, since the neighborhood can be crowded, particularly during events. Don't forget to bring your camera—the vistas are breathtaking!

Discover Destin's Boutiques & Specialty Shops

Explore Destin's lovely boutiques and specialized stores to discover hidden treasures in the retail scene. From unusual fashion discoveries and local art galleries to pleasant souvenir stores, each store is a treasure trove of one-of-a-kind goods that capture the vivid atmosphere of this seaside paradise. Prepare to embark on a shopping excursion as unique and engaging as Destin itself.

Destin's fashion stores are ideal for people who want to stand out with their flair. These shops provide a chosen collection of elegant, trendy, and coastal-inspired products, as well as a customized shopping experience that cannot be found in large chain stores.

Willow + Mercer: Located in Destin Commons, Willow + Mercer is a fashion-forward store that combines modern and boho-chic trends. From flowing dresses and attractive jumpsuits to striking accessories and contemporary footwear, this store is ideal for individuals wishing to update their wardrobe with distinctive and fashionable products.

The Dressing Room Boutique: Located in the heart of HarborWalk Village, The Dressing Room Boutique has a carefully chosen selection of fashionable apparel and accessories. Whether you're searching for a charming sundress for the beach or a stylish outfit for a night out, you'll discover a wide range of fashionable and classic designs that capture Destin's laid-back yet elegant feel.

Déjà Vu: With locations in Destin and Seaside, Déjà Vu is a popular store recognized for its feminine and flirtatious style. Déjà Vu offers a diverse assortment of items, from casual shirts and shorts to exquisite dresses and rompers, making it a must-see for fashionistas wishing to add some coastal flair to their wardrobe.

Follow these stores on social media for the most recent arrivals and specials. Don't be afraid to approach the friendly staff for style suggestions and guidance; they're eager to help you discover the right look.

Local Art Galleries: Celebrating Creativity

Destin's local art galleries provide insight into the area's thriving artistic scene. These galleries provide a broad selection of artwork from skilled local artists, making them ideal for finding one-of-a-kind items that encapsulate the beauty and spirit of Destin.

Shoreline Gallery is located in the middle of Destin and displays an eclectic mix of artworks such as paintings, sculptures, and photography. The gallery, which focuses on local and regional artists, features a diverse range of styles and materials, guaranteeing that there is something for every art fan. Take your time exploring the wonderfully selected displays and discovering a piece that calls to you.

Arts Destin Gallery: This community-driven gallery features the works of both new and experienced local artists. Arts Destin Gallery features a wide range of artworks that showcase the area's creativity and ability, including magnificent seascapes and colorful abstractions, complex ceramics, and handcrafted jewelry. The gallery also conducts seminars and events, allowing visitors to meet the artists and learn more about their work.

J.Leon Gallery and Studio: This dynamic venue combines an art gallery with functioning studios, allowing you to appreciate and purchase artwork while also watching artists at work. The gallery showcases a changing collection of paintings, glass art, and mixed-media works by local and regional artists. It's an excellent site to discover unusual artwork and learn about the creative process.

Many galleries include layaway plans and shipping alternatives, making it easy to buy and carry your desired items. Attend gallery openings and events to meet the artists and learn about their work.

Souvenir Shops: Take a Piece of Destin Home.

No vacation to Destin is complete without bringing home a unique keepsake to commemorate your journey. Destin's souvenir stores provide a lovely selection of souvenirs, ranging from traditional beach mementos to one-of-a-kind, locally crafted treasures.

Kitty Hawk Kites: Located in HarborWalk Village, Kitty Hawk Kites is a quirky business selling anything from colorful kites and beach toys to clothing and accessories. It's the ideal spot to get a colorful and whimsical keepsake that reflects the mood of your beach holiday.

Fudpucker's Beachside Gift store: Located next to the famed Fudpucker's Beachside Bar & Grill, this gift store sells a variety of gifts, including T-shirts, caps, and beach gear embossed with the classic Fudpucker's emblem. You'll also find a variety of interesting and unusual goods that would make excellent gifts for friends and family back home.

Harbor Cigars at HarborWalk Village is a great place to get a one-of-a-kind and classy keepsake. This specialist business provides a carefully chosen range of quality cigars, tobacco, and accessories. Whether you're a seasoned enthusiast or a casual smoker, the educated team can assist you in discovering the ideal cigar to enjoy and remember your trip.

For a genuinely unique and memorable memento, seek out locally manufactured products and handcrafted things. Don't be scared to approach store owners for recommendations; they usually have interesting tales and insights about their items.

Exploring Destin's boutiques and specialty stores is a lovely way to explore the seaside paradise's distinct charm and ingenuity. From stunning fashion items and intriguing artworks to unforgettable souvenirs, each business has a unique piece of Destin to give you. Put on your most comfy shoes, bring your spirit of adventure, and prepare to shop till you drop in Destin!

7.2 Destin's Markets and Festivals

Destin's bustling markets and festivals provide a true experience of the local culture, tastes, and inventiveness. These events, which range from lively weekly farmers markets bursting with fresh fruit to seasonal craft fairs exhibiting handcrafted treasures and antique stores filled with nostalgic discoveries, are ideal for immersing yourself in Destin's heart and soul. Prepare to explore, shop, and enjoy the finest that this seaside paradise has to offer!

Weekly Farmers Markets: Fresh and flavorful

Destin's weekly farmers markets are a sensory feast. These markets are brimming with fresh fruit, artisanal items, and locally manufactured delights, making them ideal for stocking up on food, finding unusual presents, and taking in the vibrant community spirit.

Destin Harbor Farmers Market: Held every Saturday in HarborWalk Village, the Destin Harbor Farmers Market is a must-see for foodies and market fans. Stroll around the colorful stalls, which sell a variety of fresh fruits and veggies, freshly baked delicacies, and locally created handicrafts. Don't miss the delectable jams, sauces, and honey, which are ideal for tasting Destin back home. Enjoy live music while shopping, making for a fun and energetic market experience.

Grand Boulevard Farmers Market: This farmers market is held every Saturday morning in the center of Sandestin's Grand Boulevard. You'll discover a variety of fresh fruit, gourmet meals, and handcrafted crafts. Sample gourmet cheeses, grab some freshly baked bread, and look through a selection of one-of-a-kind crafts and home products. The cheerful merchants are always willing to share their experiences and provide recommendations, making for a pleasant and inviting experience.

Arrive early to have the best selection, and bring reusable bags to transport your purchases. Don't be hesitant about conversing with merchants; they frequently offer wonderful ideas on how to utilize their items and can even reveal some local secrets.

Seasonal Craft Fairs: Handmade Treasures

Destin's seasonal artisan festivals celebrate creativity and craftsmanship. These fairs highlight the abilities of local artists and offer an excellent opportunity to find one-of-a-kind, handmade things that cannot be found anywhere else.

The Destin Seafood Festival, held annually in the fall, is not only a seafood lover's paradise but also a terrific artisan fair. Walk through rows of booths selling homemade jewelry, ceramics, paintings, and more. Enjoy the exciting environment, which includes live music, wonderful cuisine, and family entertainment. It's the ideal spot to shop for one-of-a-kind presents and souvenirs while enjoying the festive atmosphere.

Mattie Kelly Arts Foundation's Event of the Arts: This acclaimed arts event, held in October, is a highlight of Destin's cultural calendar. The festival has over 100 artists from throughout the country and displays a breathtaking array of fine art, including paintings, sculptures, photography, and mixed media. Take your time examining the beautifully exhibited artworks and meeting the creators behind them. It's an excellent opportunity to support the artists while also finding unique treasures for your house.

Tip: Look at the event calendar for unique activities and performances. Wear comfortable shoes and take your time exploring; there is a lot to see and appreciate. Consider carrying cash because some businesses may not take cards.

For those who like the excitement of the search, Destin's antique stores and flea markets are a treasure trove of vintage discoveries and quirky curiosities. Each visit brings a fresh discovery, whether you're looking for a rare treasure, a piece of history, or a unique keepsake.

Smith's Antiques Mall, located in Destin, is a large facility packed with booths from various antique vendors. Explore a vast assortment of furniture, home décor, jewelry, and collectibles, each with its own story. Whether you're an experienced antique collector or simply browsing, you're likely to find something interesting and unique.

De'France Indoor Flea Market & Antiques: De'France is a must-see for antique and vintage fans, located just a short drive away at Fort Walton Beach. This indoor flea market has over 100 merchants selling a wide variety of antiques, vintage things, and repurposed treasures. De'France is a great spot to spend a day exploring hidden jewels, with antique apparel and accessories, retro furniture, and one-of-a-kind knickknacks.

Shore Thing Market: Held monthly at various locations, Shore Thing Market mixes the ambiance of a flea market with the excellence of a craft show. Vendors sell a variety of handcrafted crafts, vintage treasures, and unusual antiques, making it an ideal spot to locate one-of-a-kind products. Browse the different items while enjoying the laid-back, pleasant atmosphere.

Take your time and investigate every nook and cranny; you never know what riches you may discover. Bring a list of what you're looking for, but be open to unexpected finds. Negotiate pricing, especially at flea markets.

8: Practical Information

8.1 Accommodations in Destin

Destin's beautiful beaches, exciting activities, and friendly hospitality make it a top choice for tourists looking for the ideal escape. Whether you're searching for a luxurious hideaway, a low-cost retreat, or a warm home away from home, Destin provides accommodations to fit every taste and budget. Let's look at some of the top locations to stay in this seaside paradise.

Luxury resorts: Destin's luxury resorts provide lavish lodgings, first-rate facilities, and great service to visitors looking for a genuinely magnificent vacation. Here are some noteworthy choices:

> Henderson Beach Resort: Nestled along the Gulf of Mexico's beautiful coastline, Henderson Beach Resort is an oasis of luxury and peace. This upmarket resort boasts tastefully designed rooms

and suites with breathtaking ocean views, a world-class spa, and a variety of dining options, including the well-known Primrose restaurant. Enjoy the resort's exclusive beach access, two dazzling pools, and a range of activities to soothe and thrill.

Sandestin Golf & Beach Resort: Spread over 2,400 acres, Sandestin Golf & Beach Resort provides a magnificent vacation with a variety of amenities, including beachfront condominiums and lovely villas. The resort has four championship golf courses, a marina, a fitness facility, and a spa. The Village of Baytowne Wharf offers a variety of dining, shopping, and entertainment opportunities for everyone to enjoy.

Emerald Grande at HarborWalk Village: Perched above the lively HarborWalk Village, Emerald Grande provides stunning views of the Gulf of Mexico and Destin Harbor. This premium resort offers large condominiums with complete kitchens, private balconies, and access to a full-service spa, exercise center, and beautiful pool. Because of the excellent location, you'll be only a short walk from fantastic dining, shopping, and entertainment options.

Book early to get the best greatest pricing and availability, especially during high travel seasons. Check the resort's website for special offers such as meal credits, spa treatments, and more.

Budget-Friendly Hotels: Comfortable and Affordable

Traveling on a budget does not imply abandoning comfort. Destin provides a choice of budget-friendly hotels that deliver exceptional value without sacrificing quality.

Wingate by Wyndham Destin: With its convenient location near famous activities such as Big Kahuna's Water and Adventure Park, Wingate by Wyndham provides comfortable lodgings with contemporary facilities. Guests may enjoy a free breakfast, an outdoor pool, and a fitness facility. The pleasant staff and clean, comfortable accommodations make it an excellent alternative for budget-conscious guests.

Fairfield Inn & Suites by Marriott Destin: Located within a short walk from Henderson Beach State Park, the Fairfield Inn & Suites provides an amazing value. The hotel offers spacious rooms with comfy beds, free Wi-Fi, and a daily breakfast buffet. Enjoy the hotel's outdoor pool and fitness facility, as well as its accessibility to shopping and eating options.

Holiday Inn Express & Suites Destin E - Commons Mall Area: This motel, located near Destin Commons, is both convenient and affordable. Guests may enjoy well-appointed rooms with modern facilities, a free breakfast, an outdoor pool, and a fitness center. The hotel's central position allows you to experience Destin's attractions without breaking the budget.

Look for hotels that include complimentary breakfast and parking to save even more money on your vacation. Consider reserving in the off-season for reduced prices and fewer customers.

Vacation rentals and condos are your home away from home

Consider staying in a vacation rental or apartment for a more customized and comfortable experience. Destin has a variety of alternatives, from tiny beach cottages to big condominiums with breathtaking views.

Destin Pointe Vacation Rentals: Located on the Holiday Isle, Destin Pointe has a selection of lovely beach villas and condominiums. These rentals provide all of the conveniences of a home, including fully furnished kitchens, private balconies, and access to community facilities such as pools, tennis courts, and private beaches. It's an excellent alternative for families and parties seeking a pleasant and easy getaway.

Southern Vacation Rentals: With a diverse collection of condominiums and beach villas in Destin, Southern Vacation Rentals caters to all tastes and budgets. Whether you're searching for a beachfront condo with panoramic views or a huge house with a private pool, there are plenty of possibilities to make your stay comfortable and memorable. Each house is well-maintained and well-furnished for a relaxing holiday.

Five Star Gulf Rentals specializes in luxury vacation houses and condominiums, providing top-tier residences with high-end facilities. Choose from beachfront mansions, sophisticated condominiums, and private villas, all with gorgeous designs, gourmet kitchens, and easy access to Destin's magnificent beaches. Enjoy the extra convenience of concierge services, which may arrange excursions, dinner reservations, and more.

To locate the greatest possibilities, visit trusted vacation rental websites such as VRBO, Airbnb, or local rental companies. Read reviews and look for features that matter to you, such as beach access, pet-friendliness, and Wi-Fi. Book early to obtain popular homes, especially during peak seasons.

Regardless of your budget or travel style, Destin has a variety of lodgings that promise a pleasant and pleasurable stay. From the elegance of top-tier resorts to the affordability of budget-friendly hotels and the homey feel of vacation rentals, you'll be able to discover the ideal location to call home while exploring all that this seaside paradise has to offer. So pack your luggage and go to create great moments in Destin.

8.2 Getting Around Destin

With so many transit alternatives available, you can easily navigate Destin's magnificent landscapes and bustling attractions. Whether you prefer the ease of public transportation, the flexibility of vehicle rentals, or the excitement of bicycling and scootering around town, Destin has you covered. Let's look at the finest methods to move about this seaside paradise and make the most of your vacation!

Public Transportation Options: Convenient and Environmentally Friendly

Destin has a few public transportation choices that allow you to get around without the inconvenience of driving. These services are ideal for people looking to unwind and enjoy the views while reducing their environmental impact.

Okaloosa County Transit (OCT): The OCT operates a bus service throughout Destin and the neighboring areas, giving it a handy way to move around town. The routes visit popular destinations such as Destin Commons, HarborWalk Village, and surrounding beaches. The buses are clean, comfy, and air-conditioned, which is essential in Florida's hot weather. To plan your journey, visit the OCT website and look over timetables and route maps.

Sunshine Shuttle & Limousine: For a more personalized public transportation alternative, look into Sunshine Shuttle & Limousine. They provide shuttle services to famous Destin destinations and may be scheduled ahead of time for added convenience. Whether you need a trip to the airport or a lift to your next adventure, their expert drivers will ensure smooth and comfortable travel.

To make the most of public transportation, become familiar with the bus routes and schedule. Always have cash or a transit card for bus tickets, and consider downloading the transport app for real-time updates and information.

Car rentals provide freedom and flexibility

Renting a car is one of the finest ways to experience Destin at your leisure. With a car, you may visit off-the-beaten-path beaches, attractive surrounding villages, and all of the area's attractions without following a timetable.

Enterprise Rent-A-Car: With many sites in Destin, Enterprise provides a diverse selection of automobiles to meet your needs. From modest vehicles for solitary travelers to roomy SUVs for families, you'll discover the ideal vehicle for your journey. Enterprise is well-known for providing exceptional customer service and offering convenient pick-up and drop-off locations.

Hertz: Located near the Destin-Fort Walton Beach Airport, Hertz is an easy pick for visitors traveling into town. They provide a wide range of automobiles, from economical cars to premium ones. With flexible rental dates and low pricing, Hertz makes it simple to hit the road and begin exploring as soon as you arrive.

Avis: Another excellent alternative near the airport, Avis has a varied inventory of vehicles to pick from. Whether you're planning a fast weekend break or a longer stay, Avis provides flexible rental options and high-quality automobiles to ensure a relaxing and pleasurable journey.

Reserve your vehicle rental in advance to get the best pricing and availability, especially during high travel seasons. Consider adding GPS navigation to your rental for easier exploration, and always look for any special bargains or discounts that may be available.

Bike and Scooter Rentals: Fun and Environmentally Friendly

Renting a bike or scooter is a fun and ecologically responsible way to travel to Destin. These alternatives are ideal for short outings, beach rides, and leisurely exploration of the area.

Coastal Cruisers: Located in the center of Destin, Coastal Cruisers has a diverse range of bikes, including beach cruisers, mountain bikes, and tandem cycles. They also rent electric bikes for individuals who need a little additional power. Coastal Cruisers includes helmets and locks with every rental to ensure a safe and secure trip. Explore the gorgeous bike routes, cruise along the shore, and enjoy the refreshing sea wind.

Beach Bike Rentals: Located near Henderson Beach State Park, Beach Bike Rentals provides easy access to some of Destin's top bike routes. They provide a variety of bikes for all ages and ability levels, as well as kid seats and family trailers. Take advantage of their reasonable hourly, daily, and weekly rental prices to enjoy Destin's splendor on two wheels.

Ride It Out Scooters: For a quick and fun way to move around, Ride It Out Scooters rent a selection of electric scooters. These scooters are ideal for brief journeys around town, as they are simple to use and enjoyable. Rent by the hour or the day and enjoy the ease of exploring Destin without having to worry about parking.

Always wear a helmet and obey local traffic rules, whether riding or scootering. Check the weather forecast before going out, and pack drinks and sunscreen to keep hydrated and sun-protected. Make use of Destin's dedicated bike lanes and picturesque routes to ensure a safe and pleasurable ride.

Whether you like the ease of public transportation, the independence of a rental vehicle, or the excitement of bicycling and scootering, getting around Destin is an enjoyable part of the journey. Each method of transportation provides a unique approach to exploring this stunning seaside town, allowing you to have amazing experiences at your own pace.

Stay Safe in Destin: Essential Tips for a Worry-Free Vacation.

With a little planning and knowledge, you can make sure your trip to Destin is safe and enjoyable. From beach safety to understanding local regulations and keeping emergency contacts on hand, here are some vital safety guidelines to help you make the most of your stay on Florida's Emerald Coast.

Beach safety: Enjoy the waves responsibly

Destin's lovely beaches are ideal for relaxing, playing, and soaking up the sun. To guarantee a safe and enjoyable visit, remember these beach safety tips:

Swim Near Lifeguards: Always go to a beach that has a lifeguard on duty. Lifeguards are trained to manage emergencies and can react promptly to any event. Look for approved swimming areas marked with flags or signs.

Understand the Flag System: Destin's beaches utilize flags to indicate water conditions. Green denotes calm water, yellow suggests moderate surf or currents, red indicates hazardous conditions and double red indicates that the water is restricted to the public. A purple flag warns about marine pests such as jellyfish. Always follow these instructions and swim appropriately.

Stay Hydrated and Covered: The Florida sun may be harsh, so it's critical to stay hydrated and covered. Drink lots of water throughout the day and use a broad-spectrum sunscreen with at least an SPF of 30. Reapply every two hours, after swimming or sweating. Wearing a hat and sunglasses might also offer additional protection.

Keep an eye out for marine life. Destin's seas are home to a diverse range of marine species. While encounters with deadly species are infrequent, it is prudent to exercise caution. Shuffle your feet when going in shallow water to avoid treading on stingrays, and be wary of jellyfish. When snorkeling or diving, show respect for the aquatic environment and its inhabitants.

Know Your Limits: Because the water is unpredictable, it's critical to be aware of your swimming abilities and avoid overestimating them. If you're not a good swimmer, consider wearing a life jacket and remaining in shallower water. Never swim alone; always have a companion.

Check the weather and surf forecasts before going to the beach. Keep an eye on youngsters at all times and ensure they grasp basic water safety precautions. Bring a basic first-aid kit to treat minor injuries, such as cuts and scratches.

Local Laws and Regulations: Following Destin's Rules

Understanding and observing local rules and regulations contributes to a smooth and enjoyable stay. Here are some important considerations to bear in mind:

Alcohol and Smoking: While alcohol is permitted on Destin's beaches, glass containers are forbidden to avoid accidents. To keep the beaches clean, use designated smoking locations and properly dispose of cigarette butts.

Tents, umbrellas, and other beach paraphernalia should be placed up behind the designated "line of sight" to prevent obscuring lifeguards' views. After the day, remove any personal possessions, including garbage, to help keep the beaches clean.

Fishing restrictions: If you intend to fish, ensure that you have the proper licenses and are informed of local fishing restrictions. This involves understanding the seasons, size restrictions, and bag limitations for various species. Fishing licenses may be bought online or from local bait and tackle shops.

Pets: While pets are not permitted on Destin's beaches, there are designated dog-friendly areas and parks. make your pet on a leash and clean up after them to make the environment pleasant for everyone.

Destin has noise restrictions in effect to maintain a tranquil atmosphere, particularly in residential neighborhoods. Be aware of noise levels, especially at night, and preserve the quiet of the community.

Learn the exact laws and restrictions for the beach or park you're visiting. When in doubt, ask a local or consult the official websites for the most up-to-date information. Respecting the environment and the community guarantees that everyone enjoys a positive experience.

Emergency Contacts: Be Ready for Any Situation

Having critical contact information easily available may make a significant difference in the event of an emergency. Here is a list of important contacts to keep handy:

Emergency Services: Dial 911 for police, fire, or medical emergencies. This number is your go-to for any emergency scenario that requires rapid help.

Non-Emergency Police: To report missing things or minor occurrences, call the Destin Police Department at (850) 837-8572.

Local hospitals

Ascension Sacred Heart Emerald Coast: (850) 278-3000.

Fort Walton Beach Medical Center: (850) 862-1111.

Poison Control: In the event of an accidental poisoning, call the Florida Poison Information Center at 1-800-222-1222.

Beach Safety: To learn about beach conditions, safety guidelines, and lost and found goods, call the Destin Beach Safety Office at (850) 837-4242.

For general information, recommendations, or help, contact the Destin-Fort Walton Beach Visitor Center at (800) 322-3319.

Store these numbers on your phone and maintain a paper copy in your wallet or beach bag. It's also a good idea to share this information with your fellow travelers. Knowing who to contact and where to go in an emergency may provide you peace of mind and ensure a quick response if necessary.

Currency, Tipping, and Local Etiquette: Understanding Social Customs

Destin's currency is the US dollar (USD). ATMs are commonly available, and credit cards are accepted at most places. Notify your bank of your trip intentions to avoid any card-related complications.

Tipping: Tipping is traditional in the United States and is appreciated for excellent service. In restaurants, a tip of 15% to 20% of the total cost is expected. Make sure to tip hotel employees, tour guides, and taxi drivers as well.

Local Etiquette: Embrace Destin's welcoming Southern hospitality by greeting residents with a smile and pleasant chat. When speaking with service professionals, remember to say "please" and "thank you" and to respect local customs and traditions.

Staying knowledgeable and prepared allows you to appreciate everything Destin has to offer while also ensuring a safe and worry-free visit. Whether you're relaxing on the beach, seeing local sights, or simply basking in the sun, these safety guidelines will help you make the most of your stay in this stunning coastal paradise.

As your tour of the picturesque seaside town of Destin draws to a close, it's time to reflect on your wonderful experiences and plan your next excursion. Finally, I'll cover packing basics, local etiquette, and advice for making the most of your vacation. Prepare to wrap up your vacation with confidence and passion.

Final Tips for a Smooth and Enjoyable Trip

Stay Hydrated and Protect Your Skin: The sun in Florida may be harsh, so drink lots of water and use sunscreen regularly. A wide-brimmed hat and sunglasses are also useful for sun protection.

Plan Ahead: Make reservations for popular activities, restaurants, and lodging in advance, especially during busy seasons. This helps to avoid disappointment and ensures you have the finest experiences.

Be Weather-Aware: Check the weather forecast frequently. Florida's weather may change fast, so be prepared for unexpected rain showers or temperature fluctuations.

Local Insights: Don't be afraid to ask locals for advice. They may share insider information on hidden treasures, the greatest restaurants, and off-the-beaten-path activities.

> Keep a tiny travel diary or use your phone's notes app to record your favorite destinations and experiences. This will provide you with a tailored guide for future trips, as well as suggestions for friends and family.

Packing Tips: What to Bring for a Perfect Trip

Clothing: Light, breathable textiles during the day, and a light jacket or sweater for chilly evenings. Don't forget swimsuits, flip-flops, and comfortable walking shoes.

Beach gear includes towels, a beach bag, water shoes, and a reusable water bottle. If you have the room, bring your own snorkel gear, beach umbrella, and folding chairs.

Tech and gadgets include a waterproof phone cover, a portable charger, and headphones. A decent camera, or a smartphone with a high-quality camera, is essential for recording breathtaking moments.

Health and safety supplies include a basic first aid kit, any essential prescriptions, bug repellent, and hand sanitizer. A face mask may also be effective in busy places.

Make a packing list a week before your vacation to guarantee you don't miss anything important. Review and amend the list as needed to ensure that you've covered all bases.

Etiquette and local customs: embrace the Destin way of life.

Respect the Environment: Destin's natural beauty is one of its most valuable assets. Help protect it by cleaning up after yourself, respecting wildlife, and adhering to local conservation standards.

Beach Etiquette: Keep noise levels low, especially in the early mornings and late evenings. Respect other beachgoers' space and refrain from playing loud music.

Dining Etiquette: It is typical to tip 15-20% in restaurants. If you're dining with a large party, make reservations in advance and be patient during busy periods.

Local Customs: Floridians are recognized for their warm and relaxed demeanor. A grin and a polite greeting may go a long way. Dress standards are typically casual, while certain fine dining restaurants may have strict requirements.

When visiting historical or cultural places, take the time to understand their significance and follow any restrictions or rules. Engaging with local culture enhances your trip experience.

Making the Most of Your Visit: Unlocking the Fun

Explore Beyond the Tourist Spots: While major sights are must-sees, take the time to explore lesser-known locations. To truly explore Destin, visit tiny markets, modest eateries, and secret beaches.

Try New Activities: Whether it's paddleboarding, trying a new seafood cuisine, or visiting a local festival, get out of your comfort zone and enjoy new experiences.

Capture the Moments: Take several photographs and films to document your journey. Share your trips with your friends and family, and cherish the memories.

Relax and unwind. Don't forget to take it easy and enjoy the laid-back beach atmosphere. Spend the day lazing on the beach, watching the sunset, or enjoying a spa day.

Plan a flexible schedule that incorporates must-see attractions and activities while leaving room for impromptu experiences. Sometimes the finest adventures are unplanned.

Your time in Destin will be filled with spectacular experiences, breathtaking vistas, and memorable memories. Follow these last suggestions, pack basics, and embrace local customs to guarantee a seamless and pleasant vacation. Destin's enchantment never fades, whether you're visiting for the first time or returning. So, pack your bags, enjoy the thrill, and prepare to make lifetime memories along Florida's Emerald Coast. Enjoy your travels!

Seasonal Changes to Explore: Enjoying Destin's Ever-Changing Landscape

Destin's beauty changes with the seasons, providing fresh experiences all year. Consider the following seasonal variations while planning your future trips:

Spring: Witness the blossoming of wildflowers and the return of migrant birds. In spring, the weather is great for outdoor activities like hiking, birding, and kayaking.

Summer: Celebrate the colorful energy of summer with beach days, water activities, and outdoor events. Enjoy lengthy days of sunlight and cool swims in the Gulf of Mexico.

Fall: Take in the magnificent beauty as the leaves change color and cooler temperatures come. Fall is ideal for picturesque coastal drives, nature hikes, and harvest-themed seafood festivals.

Winter: Avoid the cold and enjoy pleasant winters in Destin. Swimming may be saved for the courageous, but winter is perfect for golfing, shopping, and visiting indoor attractions such as museums and art galleries.

Visit during shoulder seasons, such as spring and fall, to avoid crowds and get better rates on hotels and activities. These seasons provide excellent weather and numerous chances for outdoor activities.

Exploring Beyond Destin

While Destin provides limitless options for adventure, the Emerald Coast is brimming with hidden gems waiting to be found. Extend your horizons by exploring nearby towns and attractions.

Scenic Drives: Take a leisurely drive along Scenic Highway 30A to explore picturesque coastal villages such as Seaside, Rosemary Beach, and Grayton Beach. Each town has its distinct appeal, including stunning architecture, boutique stores, and delectable restaurants.

State Parks: Discover the natural beauty of the Emerald Coast in adjacent state parks such as Grayton Beach State Park, Topsail Hill Preserve State Park, and St. Andrews State Park. Enjoy hiking paths, animal watching, and unspoiled beaches away from the crowds.

Day Trips: Visit ancient cities like Pensacola and Apalachicola, or take a boat cruise to explore secret coves and barrier islands. These trips provide an opportunity to learn about the Gulf Coast's rich history and unique ecology.

Cultural Events: Keep an eye out for cultural events and festivals taking place around the region. From seafood festivals and music concerts to art fairs and film festivals, there's always something spectacular going on along the Emerald Coast.

Extend your stay or plan many excursions to properly see the Emerald Coast's beauty and diversity. Every visit brings fresh experiences and opportunities for adventure.

Dreaming about Your Next Destiny Adventure

As you say goodbye to Destin, let the memories of your voyage feed your enthusiasm for future experiences. Whether you're drawn to the gorgeous beaches, the colorful culture, or the numerous outdoor activities, Destin has something for everyone. So start planning your next trip, pack your luggage, and prepare to have more wonderful experiences along Florida's Emerald Coast. Until next time, safe trip!

Printed in Great Britain
by Amazon